Integrated Series in Information Systems

Volume 32

Series Editors

Ramesh Sharda
Oklahoma State University, Stillwater, OK, USA

Stefan Voß
University of Hamburg, Hamburg, Germany

For further volumes:
http://www.springer.com/series/6157

Kun Chang Lee
Editor

Digital Creativity

Individuals, Groups, and Organizations

 Springer

Editor
Kun Chang Lee
Department of Interaction Science
Sungkyunkwan University
Seoul, Republic of South Korea

ISSN 1571-0270
ISBN 978-1-4614-5748-0   ISBN 978-1-4614-5749-7 (eBook)
DOI 10.1007/978-1-4614-5749-7
Springer New York Heidelberg Dordrecht London

Library of Congress Control Number: 2012951406

Printed on acid-free paper

Springer is part of Springer Science+Business Media (www.springer.com)

Preface

Creativity is an exciting area for both researchers and practitioners. The recent financial crisis highlighted the importance of creativity in the sense that no matter how companies tried to improve their performance, the crisis could not be avoided with conventional strategic measures. Creativity has been called a fifth management resource, following human resources, hardware resources, monetary resources, and knowledge resources. Creative products and services can turn the tide in a target market quite suddenly, transforming an underdog company into one of the most admired companies in the world. Creative strategies can impel previously hesitant consumers to open their wallets to purchase products and services in a frenzied fashion. The iPhone, produced and distributed by Apple, is a very good example of this phenomenon. Google is another example. Customers always feel a bit of nostalgia and admiration whenever they use Google services. Most of us are already addicted to using Google products and services. This phenomenon is just the tip of the iceberg in terms of what creativity can bring to companies.

The concept of creativity spans a multitude of domains, from art to science to literature to business and beyond. Even within any one context, researchers have long recognized that creativity can refer to a person, a process, a product, or an environmental response. By one count, well over 50 definitions for creativity were found, and the list continues to grow. It is easy to understand, given the wide scope of creativity, why organizations often have a difficult time capturing exactly what they mean when they strive for creative outcomes—or knowing when they have achieved them. Current definitions of cognitive creativity (e.g., scientific or organizational) typically describe the construct as involving "the generation of novel behavior that meets a standard of quality or utility." Traditionally, this is accomplished by research and development scientists through qualitative means such as fluency, flexibility, and originality. Quantitatively, it is measured by item counts in brainstorming lists, numbers of patent applications, and citation counts.

As digital innovation has permeated our daily lives and become part of our environment, creativity has started to take a new shape compared to its past form—digital creativity. The Internet has changed everything we know. Web technologies and the related dazzling advancements have drastically altered our living patterns, affecting the way we shop, how we receive health care, our choice of entertainment, the methods we use to vote, the officiating and broadcasting of sports, educational delivery techniques, and more. Without exception, all the realms of our lives are now influenced by a wide variety of digital technologies such as the Internet.

Similarly, one would expect that studies about creativity would also have been influenced by the Internet. Surprisingly, however, sufficient attention has not been paid to how the Internet and related digital technologies have changed all the aspects of creativity—the source of creativity, the process of revealing creativity, team creativity, and organizational creativity. A typical example of how digital technology influences creativity is social networking, where individuals connected to others online can access a more plentiful supply of relevant information than ever, enabling them to focus on target issues and themes more effectively. Even companies have become more creative in locating potentially loyal customers by using digital technologies that provide excellent data mining mechanisms, enabling companies to search for target customers with high effectiveness and efficiency.

Summarizing all the arguments so far, now is the time for us to consider the potential influence of digital technologies on creativity. Now, with Internet usage so prevalent, many types of technology jumping out of the lab and becoming ubiquitous, and all kinds of digital devices available on the market and at home, it is the perfect time to discuss digital creativity, which is defined as all forms of creativity driven by digital technologies. In this book, we will discuss the vast influence that digital technologies have on creativity from the individual level to the team level and all the way to the organizational level. This book proposes a new kind of creativity model encompassing all levels of creativity—individual, team, and organizational. These three levels of creativity should, ideally, be combined into a unified creativity framework in which organizations, regardless of their industry, benefit by re-engineering their business processes and strategies. Toward that end, this book considers various factors that affect creativity, including individuals' digital efficacy, heterogeneity among team members (i.e., demographics such as age, gender, race, tenure, education, and culture), computer-mediated communication (CMC), task complexity, exploitation, exploration, culture, organizational learning capability, and knowledge networks among members.

The influence of digital creativity is reshaping the way individuals, teams, and modern organizations operate. Although creativity has been studied for many years by organizational researchers, as digital technologies such as the Internet become established as the standard tools for communications, work, and entertainment delivery, the conventional definition of creativity needs to be redefined and reinterpreted from the perspective of digital technology. When information is digitized into a stream of bits, it is easily distributed through computer networks, becoming accessible through the Internet to any person who needs it, thus increasing its value tremendously.

By using a wide variety of digital technologies, individuals can stimulate their own untapped creativity. Individuals who were previously isolated from the creative influences of cultural and educational opportunities by distance or circumstance can now nourish themselves with the rich supply of information available from the borderless and seemingly limitless digital world powered by the Internet. Teams that had to work on their own before the digital age, communicating with outside teams in only a very limited way, can now work in a truly networked fashion, connecting to other teams, persons and organizations through digital networks. Organizations that were previously confined to searching for valuable resources through outside agencies that were often notorious for their poor quality of service are now free to use digital technologies to pursue any purpose they want. In a word, now is the time for individuals, teams, and organizations to harness the power of digital creativity, and they can do so if only they have the will.

This book introduces a theoretical and systematic glimpse into the exciting realm of digital creativity. To help keep readers interested and motivated all the way to the end of the book, I have organized the contents by focusing initially on individuals and then progressing to teams and ultimately to organizations, highlighting specific techniques and cases along the way. Each chapter will show you how individuals, teams and organizations can become creative through digital technologies. Individual creativity is discussed through Chaps. 1–6. Creativity in teams and organizations is investigated in Chaps. 7 and 8. At the end of book, I introduce two chapters (Chaps. 9 and 10) showing the possible directions of future studies regarding creativity. Chapter summaries are as follows.

Chapter Summaries

Chapter 1 discusses the effects of team member exchange (TMX) and coworker helping and support (CHS) on individual creativity. Job stress was considered to be a negative antecedent of creativity, and researchers hypothesized that TMX and CHS would decrease job stress within Korean Information and Communication Technology (ICT) companies. It was found that although CHS does not have a sufficient effect on individual creativity, it is positively related to individual creativity. TMX, on the other hand, was found to directly and strongly influence individual creativity, and job stress was found to negatively influence individual creativity.

Chapter 2 is concerned with investigating the relationship between stress and performance. A computer game was used as a way of sharing common features with computer-mediated tasks under manipulated job-related stress conditions. Respondents were divided into two groups: the stress-manipulated group and the non-stress group. During the experiments, each group was measured using galvanic skin response (GSR) technology and by electrocardiogram (ECG) to ascertain the level of stress. The experiment results showed insignificant differences between the control group (non-stress) and the manipulated group (stress) in performing the computer-mediated tasks.

Chapter 3 It is widely known that modern companies try to enhance their digital creativity to more firmly establish their competitiveness in the marketplace. The purpose of Chap. 3 is to longitudinally explore the evolutionary pattern of digital creativity to explain how communication effectiveness, task expertise, and the tendencies of digitalists affect digital creativity, with a focus on task diversity. Using multi-agent simulation (MAS) on the NetLogo platform, it was proved that these elements help form a valid model for digital creativity.

Chapter 4 In this study, a physiological approach was employed to study the relationship between stress and creativity using a controlled experiment. For the sake of the experiment, participants were categorized into a stress group and a non-stress group. The experiment results revealed that self-reported creativity did not correspond with an assessment by experts of participants' creativity. Also, there was no statistically significant relationship between stress and creativity, indicating that other factors may play a role and further studies are necessary in this respect.

Chapter 5 explores the revelation process for individual creativity based on exploitation and exploration. The purpose of this chapter is to investigate how task difficulty and emotion, as sources of stress, affect creativity manifestation activities such as exploration and exploitation in the decision support system environment. During the experiment, a specific situation was presented to the participants where the subjects needed to exert creativity to accomplish a task, and the result was analyzed through the measurement of physiological signal data as the subjects attempted to complete the task. The empirical results revealed that exploration activities are facilitated in less stressful environments and that exploitation is facilitated in stressful situations.

Chapter 6 proposes an individual creativity model that consists of personal psychological characteristics and creative processes. To test the model, researchers investigated how emotional and social intelligence positively, effectively, and successfully lead to harmonized human relationships in the existing social order, affecting the creative process and individual creativity. This chapter is particularly concerned with understanding how exploration and exploitation are related to personal psychological characteristics and individual creativity. Survey analysis results showed that personal psychological characteristics, measured by social and emotional intelligence, significantly affect the creative process and individual creativity. Another interesting finding is that exploration reinforces individual creativity whereas exploitation does not directly strengthen individual creativity.

Chapter 7 explores the issue of team creativity by using a unique intelligent method known as a Bayesian network. It is generally understood that team creativity influences corporate performance in a decisive manner, and improving it significantly is at the heart of most strategies. Accordingly, organizations have been concerned not only with fostering creativity and innovation among individual employees, but also with developing creative and innovative teams. However, when it comes to enhancing the level of team creativity, decision makers are embarrassed and even intimidated by the huge number of relevant factors waiting to be analyzed and the degree of complexity of the causal relationships existing among them. To address that obstacle, this chapter proposes useful management methods for improving team creativity by performing a variety of scenario-based sensitivity analyses based on a General Bayesian Network (GBN). More specifically, this study proposes a GBN-driven approach to effectively managing team creativity, in which five variables—exploration, exploitation, knowledge sharing, expertise heterogeneity, and organizational learning culture—are handled in the context of causal relationships with team creativity.

Chapter 8 is unique in that it investigates the effects of network structure-related factors on team creativity. The network structure factors under consideration include heterogeneity, degree centrality, and structural holes among various contextual and social factors that affect team creativity. In addition, this chapter focuses on the longitudinal evolution patterns of team creativity to address how the effects of heterogeneity and the network structure change over time. The main method adopted is an agent-based modeling (ABM) approach, which was used to longitudinally analyze the change and evolution patterns of team creativity. It was found that the network structure, particularly the elements of degree centrality and structural holes, is more effective in improving team creativity than heterogeneity over the long term, although both heterogeneity and network structure positively affect team creativity.

Chapter 9 examines the effect of short-term robot-mediated training for creativity education. Individual creativity was measured in terms of creative self-efficacy and creative outcome. In the study, some of the participants were allowed to play with the robot, and their creativity was compared with other groups who either just watched robot-related movie clips or designed the robot's behavior. The results showed an improvement in creative self-efficacy among the participants who designed the robot's behavior.

Chapter 10 explores the interrelationship between creativity, technology, and social practices. It is clear that continual exploration is necessary for us to shape and transform our practices in a rapidly changing and intensely complex world, thus digital creativity is crucial. This chapter examines how digital creativity is transforming our practices—what we know, how we act, and who we are becoming. It is this continuum—the interrelationship between the creativity of action and the digital world—that is reconfiguring social practices in new and critical ways.

Seoul, Republic of South Korea   Kun Chang Lee

Acknowledgments

It has been my great pleasure to have an exciting chance to work with the editorial team at Springer US. Matthew Amboy and Neil Levine, who are now (associate) editors and my main contact at Springer US, were top quality professionals I have ever worked with. They have been indeed a main source of advice and help for this project. I likewise very much appreciate the contributions of Youngwook Seo, Sungwook Chae, Namyong Jo, Daesung Lee, Minhee Hahn, Doyoung Choi, Jungsik Hwang, and Teresa Swirski to this project.

Finally, my profound thanks go to my wife Sun-Yang, and my daughter Eun-Sung, two sons Jae-Sung and Min-Sung. You were always an amazing source of encouragements and enlightenments for me during doing this project. My deep gratitude also goes to the National Research Foundation of Korea for their generous financial support to this project with grant (KRF-2009-342-B00015) and WCU (World-Class University) research fund (Grant No. R31-2008-000-10062-0).

I hope that this book may shed novel guidelines for both scholars and practitioners who seek to add more brand new ideas and insights to what they have been pursuing so far to take advantage of creativity studies in their ongoing jobs.

Seoul, Republic of South Korea   Kun Chang Lee

Contents

Chapter 1
Creativity and Job Stress in the Korean ICT Industry: TMX and CHS as Antecedents

Dae Sung Lee, Kun Chang Lee, and Nam Yong Jo

1.1 Introduction

In order to increase their adaptability and growth, many organizations have considered creativity as the building block for organizational innovation in the global competitive business environment [54]. The ubiquity of communication devices such as telephones, computers, television, and radio indicates that Information and Communication Technologies (ICTs) are fast becoming essential components of our day-to-day lives. Therefore, we need to examine employee creativity in ICT industries that require a high level of organizational creativity. Research by Amabile and associates shows the value of investigating the creativity of individuals and groups within their relevant social settings [30]. *The interactionist model of creativity* [55, 56] emphasizes the social influences of groups and contextual influences of organizations, both of which affect individual and team creativity. In this respect, we included team member exchange (TMX) and coworker helping and support (CHS) as social/contextual factors in our model because they may impact individual creativity within an organization. We also considered job stress as a negative antecedent of creativity in the model. Previous studies have demonstrated negative, positive, and curvilinear relationships between stress and

D.S. Lee • N.Y. Jo
SKK Business School, Sungkyunkwan University, Seoul 110-745, Republic of Korea
e-mail: leeds1122@gmail.com; namyong.jo@gmail.com

K.C. Lee (✉)
Department of Interaction Science, SKK Business School, Sungkyunkwan University,
Seoul 110-745, Republic of South Korea
e-mail: kunchanglee@gmail.com

K.C. Lee (ed.), *Digital Creativity: Individuals, Groups, and Organizations*,
Integrated Series in Information Systems 32, DOI 10.1007/978-1-4614-5749-7_1,
© Springer Science+Business Media New York 2013

1

creativity. Inasmuch as the stress imposed by intense workload pressures may undermine an employee's creativity in an organization [2, 22], we examined the negative relationship between job stress and creativity. Many researchers have emphasized that social support has a positive or buffering effect on social relationships in the workplace [26, 33], so social relationships in the workplace may effectively decrease job stress. Additionally, we investigated the negative effects of TMX and CHS on job stress. Although some researchers have examined the relationship between leader member exchange (LMX) and employee creativity, few have examined the effects of TMX on creativity. Thus, we contribute to the literature on the relationship between social exchange relationships and creativity.

1.2 Theoretical Background and Hypotheses

1.2.1 Individual Creativity Within Organizations

Creativity may be defined as the ability to produce work that is both novel and useful [37, 49]. If this concept is placed within an organization, organizational creativity is that which yields a valuable, useful new idea, product, service, procedure, or process by individuals working together in a complex social system [55]. Researchers need to investigate the creative product, process, person, and situation in order to understand organizational creativity. Above all, it is necessary to understand how each of these components interacts with the others [9, 23].

In the interactionist model of organizational creativity, Woodman and colleagues [55, 56] argued that individual creativity requires antecedent conditions, including cognitive styles and abilities, personality, motivational factors, and knowledge [30]. These individual factors are both influenced by, and influence, the social and contextual factors in the model. When individual creativity occurs, social influences on individual creativity are immediately established in the group, with the two influencing each other [55]. Group creativity is not the simple aggregate of all group members' creativity, although group creativity is clearly a function of the creativity of the individuals in the group. Group creativity is also influenced by factors representing group features, such as group composition, characteristics, processes (e.g., diversity, cohesiveness, group size, problem-solving strategies, social information processes), and contextual influences [55]. Based on the *interactionist model of creativity*, we emphasize social settings in organizations and select TMX and CHS as social and contextual factors that may influence individual creativity within an organization.

1.2.2 Job Stress

Early researchers on work stress explored features of the physical work environment or the physical and cognitive demands of work tasks [43]. However, many researchers have since focused on the psychosocial dimensions of the work environment and work tasks by conceptualizing work stress as a form of role stress [35]. The most influential framework is the "demand-control" model of job strain [27, 28]. This model identifies the salient dimensions of job conditions, including the level of demands and degree of control or decision latitude that workers exercise [40]. Demands and control have interactive effects on job stress. "High-strain" jobs require high demands and low control, and these types of jobs are the most stressful for workers. Many studies have found that workers in high-strain jobs are at greater risk for various health problems and psychological distress [27, 28, 41]. In an effort to elaborate the demand-control model, researchers have placed greater emphasis on the social environment of work [41, 51]. The elaboration of this paradigm was enabled by two empirical findings: the importance of social support from supervisors and coworkers [26], and changes in the occupational structure of industrial societies [33].

1.2.3 Creativity and Stress

The existing literature shows the effect of stress on performance as an inverted U-shaped (curvilinear) relationship. This suggests that some degree of stress helps workers maintain concentration on a task through excitement. Incidentally, a review of previous studies on the relationship between stress and creativity confirms the existence of negative, positive, and curvilinear relationships between the two.

In view of distraction arousal theory [53], stress has a negative effect on creativity performance. People pay attention to stress with some of these resources due to limited mental resources, employing fewer cognitive resources for other tasks [11]. This generally leads to simpler cognitive strategies, such as using a narrower attentional focus [16], and these simple cognitive strategies generate more common, less original ideas [8, 14]. Therefore, people employ simpler cognitive strategies that may undermine creativity [11]. On the other hand, some theories suggest that stress has a positive effect on creativity because stress elicits creative thoughts and motivates people to solve problems (e.g., [4, 36]). In short, if individuals are exposed to stress, they may use problem-solving strategies, enhancing creativity [10]. Hence, stress is, from this viewpoint, positively related to creativity because it brings about creative solutions and motivates creative thinking [5, 38]. By summing up the positive and negative influences, some researchers have proposed that stress is curvilinearly related to creativity (e.g., [57]). Activation theory (e.g., [20]) posits that stress can enhance performance only to a threshold, but too much activation restricts performance, particularly for complex tasks such as those requiring creativity [6]. A moderate level of activation may prompt individuals to be their most creative. The moderate activation level increases task engagement and leads to the optimal use of cognitive resources by lowering negative affect (e.g., [7, 20]). Too little or too much activation may bring about a lack of engagement and cognitive interference. Given that cognitive, emotional, and behavioral engagement are important processes for creativity [13], a moderate level of activation leads to the most creativity [11].

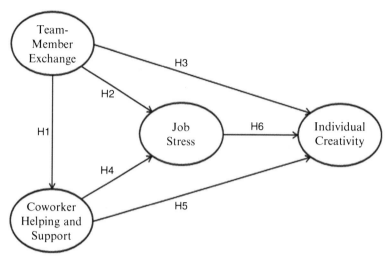

Fig. 1.1 Research model

1.2.4 Selected Antecedents and Hypotheses

1.2.4.1 Team Member Exchange

Seers [45] defined TMX as a way to assess the reciprocity between a member and his or her team [32]. In this definition, TMX represents the quality of team members' working relationships with their peer group; the quality is measured by a member's willingness to assist team members, share feedback, and contribute ideas [29, 45]. Seers et al. [46] found that TMX was higher in autonomous teams than traditional work groups. In other words, the more a group self manages, the greater the need for members to be engaged in supportive reciprocal exchanges with one another [46]. On the basis of these studies, we proposed our first hypothesis.

Hypothesis 1:Team member exchange will positively *contribute to coworker help and support.*
House [26] emphasized the importance of social support from supervisors and coworkers in reducing job stress. Moreover, other researchers (e.g., [43, 51, 52]) have incorporated relationships with coworkers or supervisors into the "demand-control" model on job stress. High-quality TMX allows a team member to sufficiently interact with other members. As TMX is considered as reciprocal relations with coworkers within the model, low-strain jobs (low demands and high control) are consequently less stressful for workers. On the basis of these studies, we proposed Hypothesis 2.

Hypothesis 2: Team member exchange will negatively *contribute to job stress.*
Individual creativity is often enacted in a team context [47], so it is necessary to theoretically and empirically understand how a member's social exchange relationships with other members influence that individual's creativity. High-quality TMX allows a team member to sufficiently interact with other members, heeding their work behavior and expressed ways of thinking [31]. Therefore, TMX may be a social factor that influences creativity. On the basis of these studies, we proposed Hypothesis 3.

Hypothesis 3: Team member exchange will positively *contribute to individual creativity.*

1.2.4.2 Coworker Helping and Support

Coworker support is defined as "the extent to which employees believe their coworkers are willing to provide them with work-related assistance to aid in the execution of their service-based duties" (Susskind et al. 2003, p. 181) [50]. CHS involve situations where coworkers help another employee with tasks by sharing knowledge and expertise or providing encouragement and support. Many researchers have emphasized that social support has a positive or buffering effect on social relationships in the workplace [26, 33]. Essentially, holding a low-strain job with good social support might be negatively related to job stress. On the basis of these studies, we proposed Hypothesis 4.

Hypothesis 4: Coworker helping and support will negatively *contribute to job stress.*

If coworkers are helpful and supportive, it would not be relatively difficult for employees to use their coworkers as a catalyst for new ideas [18, 44]. On the basis of these studies, we proposed a fifth hypothesis.

Hypothesis 5: Coworker helping and support will positively *contribute to individual creativity.*

1.2.4.3 Job Stress

For the purpose of our study, stress is defined as distress, or stress that has reached a level at which it has negative effects on cognitive performance, such as on a creative task. Existing studies have proposed that the stress imposed by intense workload pressures may undermine an employee's creativity in organizations [2, 22]. Moreover, Amabile et al. [3] suggested that workload and time pressures combined with frequent interruptions can reduce employees' creativity by almost half. In this respect [6], job stress might be negatively related to employee creativity. On the basis of these studies, we proposed a sixth hypothesis.

Hypothesis 6: Job stress will negatively *contribute to individual creativity.*

Table 1.1 Sample characteristics

Characteristics		Frequency	Percent
Gender	Male	259	80.9
	Female	61	19.1
Age	19–29	92	28.8
	30–39	185	57.8
	40–49	42	13.1
	50–59	1	0.3
Position	Assistant	63	19.7
	Senior assistant	100	31.3
	Manager	86	26.9
	Senior manager	71	22.2
Job	IT planning	50	15.6
	Analysis for client requirements	40	12.5
	IT analysis	20	6.3
	IT consulting	55	17.2
	R&D	84	26.3
	System analysis	32	10.0
	Others	39	12.2

Total number of respondents is 320

1.3 Research Methodology

1.3.1 Data Collection

The participants were employees of Korean ICT companies. We paid a survey company to collect a total of 365 surveys. To avoid selection bias, inconsistent or incomplete responses were eliminated from the dataset. Respondents who were in higher positions than senior managers (directors or executives) were also excluded because our questionnaire was designed for employees who horizontally interact with each other. This process yielded 320 useable cases (87.7 %). Table 1.1 reports the sample characteristics.

1.3.2 Measures

We measured each item in our model on a seven-point Likert scale, with answers ranging from one (strongly disagree) to seven (strongly agree; see Table 1.2). The items in the survey were developed by adapting existing measures validated by previous studies or by converting construct definitions into a questionnaire format.

Table 1.2 Construct and measurement

Construct	Items	Measurement	Related literature
Team-member exchange	TMX1	I am flexible about switching jobs with others in my work group.	Seers [17]
	TMX2	Other group members recognize my potential.	
	TMX3	Other group members understand my problems.	
	TMX4	I am willing to finish work assigned to others.	
	TMX5	Others are willing to finish work assigned to me.	
Coworker helping and support	CHS1	My coworkers willingly share their expertise with each other.	Podsakoff et al. [39]
	CHS2	My coworkers help each other out if someone falls behind in his/her work.	
	CHS3	My coworkers encourage each other when someone is down.	
	CHS4	My coworkers try to act like peacemakers when there are disagreements.	
Job stress	S1	Your job makes you upset.	Sosik and Godshalk [48]
	S2	Your job makes you frustrated.	
	S3	You are under strain on the job.	
	S4	Your job makes you jumpy and nervous.	
	S5	Your job puts you under a lot of pressure.	
Individual creativity	IC1	I am willing to propose a new idea or method ahead of my coworkers.	Ettlie O'Keefe [15], Scott and Bruce [44], Zhou and George [58]
	IC2	I generally use existing methods and instruments as new ones.	
	IC3	I employ a proper planning and scheduling in order to implement a new idea.	
	IC4	I propose a new and better method to achieve a goal.	

1.4 Results

1.4.1 Measurement

Partial least squares (PLS) analysis has been widely used in theory testing and confirmation, and is appropriate for determining whether relationships are positive or negative [19]. We employed SmartPLS 2.0 to analyze the measurement and structural models. As shown in Table 1.3, our composite reliability values ranged from 0.896 to 0.924, and our variance extracted by the measures ranged from 0.632 to 0.727. All of these figures are above acceptable levels. The discriminant validity was assessed by examining the correlations among variables [19]. For satisfactory discriminant validity, the average variance extracted (AVE) from the construct should be greater than the variance shared between the construct and other constructs in the model [12]. Table 1.4 lists the correlation matrix with the correlations among the constructs and the square root of the AVE on the diagonal.

Table 1.3 Confirmatory factor analysis

Construct	Items	Factor loading	t-value	Cronbach's α	Composite reliability	AVE
Team-member exchange	TMX1	0.717	20.498	0.855	0.896	0.632
	TMX2	0.812	36.887			
	TMX3	0.839	44.631			
	TMX4	0.827	40.826			
	TMX5	0.775	21.335			
Coworker helping and support	CHS1	0.824	34.266	0.860	0.906	0.707
	CHS2	0.878	47.151			
	CHS3	0.893	69.258			
	CHS4	0.763	19.217			
Job stress	S1	0.725	4.406	0.909	0.924	0.711
	S2	0.872	6.414			
	S3	0.812	6.128			
	S4	0.930	5.978			
	S5	0.864	5.828			
Individual creativity	IC1	0.862	52.316	0.874	0.914	0.727
	IC2	0.758	17.747			
	IC3	0.888	64.343			
	IC4	0.896	80.784			

Table 1.4 Correlation of latent variables

Construct	Team-member exchange	Coworker helping and support	Job stress	Individual creativity
Team-member exchange	0.795			
Coworker helping and support	0.677	0.841		
Job stress	−0.072	−0.044	0.843	
Individual creativity	0.532	0.468	−0.148	0.853

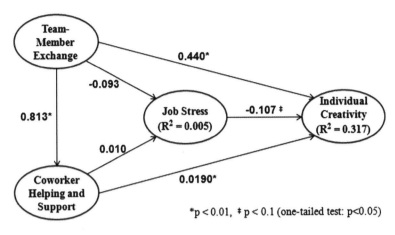

Fig. 1.2   Research model results

Table 1.5 Results of the hypothesis tests

Hypotheses	Path	Coefficient (β)	t-value
H1	Team-member exchange → coworker helping and support	0.813	20.678*
H2	Team-member exchange → job stress	−0.093	0.777
H3	Team-member exchange → individual creativity	0.440	13.600*
H4	Coworker helping and support → job stress	0.010	0.106
H5	Coworker helping and support → individual creativity	0.190	2.636*
H6	Job stress → individual creativity	−0.107	1.701‡

*$p<0.01$, ‡$p<0.1$ (one-tailed test: $p<0.05$)

1.4.2   Structural Model

We tested the structural model by estimating the path coefficients and R^2 values, both of which indicate how well the data support the hypothesized model. Figure 1.2 and Table 1.5 present the results of the test of the hypothesized structural model. The R^2 value (0.317) for individual creativity in this model is above the value of 10 % recommended by Falk and Miller [17]. However, the R^2 value (0.005) for job stress is below the recommended value. This leads us to reject H2 and H3 in this model, as shown in Table 1.5. All other hypotheses in the model are supported. Nonetheless, the strengths of the paths vary in terms of the coefficient levels. The findings of the present study are discussed in the section below.

1.5 Discussion

1.5.1 Implications

We cannot statistically confirm the effects of TMX or CHS on job stress. All workplace relationships are not positive [42]. Some researchers have focused on the interpersonal dynamics of service work as a source of work stress [21, 33], which suggests that social support and interactions among team members may bring about job stress for some employees, but not for others. Although CHS does not have a sufficient effect on individual creativity aside from statistical significance, it positively contributes to individual creativity.

From the results, we found that TMX directly and strongly influences individual creativity, and job stress has a negative impact on individual creativity (one-tailed test: $p < 0.05$). As a contextual factor, the concept of TMX is broader than that of coworkers' other behaviors (such as CHS) in that TMX represents the intention to help teammates, share feedback, and contribute ideas [45]. Therefore, managers should pay attention to social exchange relationships such as TMX and improve work environments in order to enhance individual creativity within an organization.

1.5.2 Limitations and Future Research

Our study targeted only Korean ICT companies, and future researchers should pursue comparative studies in various industries. We likely did not consider many important antecedents of TMX, and future researchers should also focus on identifying different types of justice, team temporal scope, communication mediation, and supervisor-subordinate relationships as antecedents of TMX (e.g., [1, 24]). On the other hand, we did not fully explain the effects of TMX and CHS on job stress. Hochschild's [25] study of conceptualized emotional labor has inspired many subsequent studies of job stress in service occupations. As the significance of emotional labor has been acknowledged in a variety of occupations [34], it is necessary to multilaterally investigate the effects of interpersonal dynamics and emotional factors on job stress among Korean ICT companies. In other words, we need to sufficiently examine positive and negative effects on job stress in organizations and further investigate the various antecedents of such stress. Finally, we did not consider many important antecedents of creativity, and future researchers should explore how personal traits (such as age, level of education, and working experience), diversity within a team, and organizational characteristics (such as firm size and industry type) moderate the relationships among the constructs.

Acknowledgment This work was supported by the Korea Research Foundation Grant funded by the Korean Government (KRF-2009-342-B00015).

References

1. Alge, B.J., Wiethoff, C., Klein, H.J.: When does the medium matter? Knowledge-building experience and opportunities in decision making teams. Organ. Behav. Hum. Decis. Process. **91**(1), 26–37 (2003)
2. Amabile, T.M., Conti, R., Coon, H., Lazenby, J., Herron, M.: Assessing the work environment for creativity. Acad. Manage. J. **39**(5), 1154–1184 (1996)
3. Amabile, T.M., Hadley, C.N., Kramer, S.J.: Creativity under the gun. Harv. Bus. Rev. **80**(8), 52–61 (2002)
4. Anderson, N., De Dreu, C.K.W., Nijstad, B.A.: The routinization of innovation research: A constructively critical review of the State-of-the-science. J. Organ. Behav. **25**(2), 147–173 (2004)
5. Andrews, F.M., Farris, G.F.: Time pressure and performance of scientists and engineers: A five-year panel study. Organ. Behav. Hum. Decis. Process. **8**(2), 185–200 (1972)
6. Avey, J.B., Luthans, F., Hannah, S.T., Sweetman, D., Peterson, C.: Impact of employees' character strengths of wisdom on stress and creative performance. Hum. Resource. Manage. J. (2011). doi:doi: 10.1111/j.1748-8583.2010.00157.x
7. Baer, M., Oldham, G.R.: The curvilinear relation between experienced creative time pressure and creativity: Moderating effects of openness to experience and support for creativity. J. Appl. Psychol. **91**(4), 963–970 (2006)
8. Baron, R.S.: Distraction-conflict theory: Progress and problems. Adv. Exp. Soc. Psychol. **19**, 1–39 (1986)
9. Brown, R.T.: Creativity: What are we to measure? In: Glover, A., Ronning, R.R., Reynolds, C.R. (eds.) Handbook of Creativity, pp. 3–32. Plenum Press, New York (1989)
10. Bunce, D., West, M.: Changing work environments, innovative coping responses to occupational stress. Work Stress **8**(4), 319–331 (1994)
11. Byron, K., Khazanchi, S., Nazarian, D.: The relationship between stressors and creativity: A meta-analysis examining competing theoretical models. J. Appl. Psychol. **95**(1), 201–212 (2010)
12. Chin, W.W.: The partial least squares approach to structural equation modeling. In: Marcoulides, G.A. (ed.) Modern Methods for Business Research. Lawrence Erlbaum, Mahway, NJ (1988)
13. Drazin, R., Glynn, M.A., Kazanjian, R.K.: Multilevel theorizing about creativity in organizations: A sensemaking perspective. Acad. Manage. Rev. **24**(2), 286–307 (1999)
14. Drwal, R.L.: The Influence of psychological stress upon creative thinking. Pol. Psychol. Bull. **4**, 125–129 (1973)
15. Ettlie, J.E., O'Keefe, R.D.: Innovative attitudes, values, and intentions in organizations. J. Manage. Stud. **19**(2), 163–182 (1982)
16. Eysenck, H.J.: Genius: The Natural History of Creativity. Cambridge University Press, Cambridge, MA (1995)
17. Falk, R.F., Miller, N.B.: A Premier for Soft Modeling. The University of Akron, Akron, OH (1992)
18. Farr, J.L.: Facilitating individual role innovation. In: West, M.A., Farr, J.L. (eds.) Innovation and Creativity at Work: Psychological and Organizational Strategies, pp. 207–230. Wiley, Oxford, England (1990)
19. Fornell, C.R., Lacker, D.F.: Two structural equation models with unobservable variables and measurement error. J. Market. Res. **18**(1), 39–50 (1981)
20. Gardner, D.G.: Activation theory and task design: An empirical test of several new predictions. J. Appl. Psychol. **71**(3), 411–418 (1986)
21. Hall, E.M.: Gender, work control, and stress: A theoretical discussion and an empirical test. In: Johnson, J., Johansson, G. (eds.) The Psychosocial Work Environment: Work Organization, Democratization and Health, pp. 89–108. Baywood, Amityville, NY (1991)
22. Hallowell, E.M.: Overloaded circuits. Why smart people underperform. Harv. Bus. Rev. **83**(1), 54–62 (2005)

23. Harrington, D.M.: The ecology of human creativity: A psychological perspective. In: Runco, M.A., Albert, R.S. (eds.) Theories of Creativity, pp. 143–169. Sage, Newbury Park, CA (1990)

24. Hiller, N.J., Day, D.V.: LMX and teamwork: The challenges and opportunities of diversity. In: Graen, G.B. (ed.) Dealing with Diversity: A Volume in LMX Leadership: The Series, vol. 1, pp. 29–57. Information Age Publishing, Greenwich, CT (2003)

25. Hochschild, A.R.: The Managed Heart: The Commercialization of Human Feeling. University of California Press, Berkeley (1983)

26. House, J.S.: Work Stress and Social Support. Addison-Wesley, Palo Alto, CA (1981)

27. Karasek, R.A.: Job demands, job decision latitude and mental strain: Implications for Job redesign. Admin. Sci. Q. **24**(2), 285–308 (1979)

28. Karasek, R.A.: Lower health risk with increased job control among white collar workers. J. Organ. Behav. **11**(3), 171–185 (1990)

29. Kluger, A.N., DeNisi, A.: The effects of feedback interventions on performance: A historical review, a meta-analysis, and a preliminary feedback intervention theory. Psychol. Bull. **119**(2), 254–284 (1996)

30. Lee, D.S., Seo, Y.W., Lee, K.C.: Individual and team differences in self-reported creativity by shared leadership and individual knowledge in an e-learning environment. Information **14**(9), 2931–2946 (2011)

31. Liao, H., Liu, D., Loi, R.: Looking at both sides of the social exchange coin: A social cognitive perspective on the joint effects of relationship quality and differentiation on creativity. Acad. Manage. J. **53**(5), 1090–1109 (2010)

32. Liu, Y., Keller, R.T., Shih, H.A.: The impact of team-member exchange, differentiation, team commitment, and knowledge sharing on R&D project team performance. R&D Manage. **41**(3), 274–287 (2011)

33. MacDonald, C.L., Sirianni, C.: The service society and the changing experience of work. In: MacDonald, C.L., Sirianni, C. (eds.) Working in the Service Society, pp. 1–26. Temple University Press, Philadelphia (1996)

34. Morris, J.A., Feldman, D.C.: The dimensions, antecedents, and consequences of emotional labor. Acad. Manage. Rev. **21**(4), 986–1010 (1996)

35. Newton, T.: "Managing" Stress: Emotion and Power at Work. Sage Publications, London (1995)

36. Nicol, J.J., Long, B.C.: Creativity and perceived stress of female music therapists and hobbyists. Creativ. Res. J. **9**(1), 1–10 (1996)

37. Oldham, G.R., Cummings, A.: Employee creativity: Personal and contextual factors at work. Acad. Manage. J. **39**(3), 607–634 (1996)

38. Pelz, D.C.: Creative tensions in the research and development climate. In: Katz, R. (ed.) Managing Professionals in Innovative Organizations: A Collection of Readings, pp. 37–48. Ballinger, New York (1988)

39. Podsakoff, P.M., Ahearne, M., MacKenzie, S.B.: Organizational citizenship behavior and the quantity and quality of work group performance. J. Appl. Psychol. **82**(2), 262–270 (1997)

40. Pugliesi, K.: The consequences of emotional labor: Effectson work stress, job satisfaction, and well-being. Motiv. Emot. **23**(2), 125–154 (1999)

41. Radmacher, S.A., Sheridan, C.L.: An investigation of the demand-control model of job strain. In: Sauter, S.L., Murphy, L.R. (eds.) Organizational Risk Factors for Job Stress, pp. 127–138. American Psychological Association, Washington, DC (1995)

42. Richman, J.A., Rospenda, K.M., Nawyn, S.J., Flaherty, J.A.: Workplace harassment and the self-medication of distress: A conceptual model and case illustrations. Contemp. Drug Probl. **24**, 179–200 (1997)

43. Sauter, S.L., Murphy, L.R.: The changing face of work and stress. In: Sauter, S.L., Murphy, L.R. (eds.) Organizational Risk Factors for Job Stress, pp. 1–6. American Psychological Association, Washington, DC (1995)

44. Scott, S.G., Bruce, R.A.: Determinants of innovative behavior: A path model of individual innovation in the workplace. Acad. Manage. J. **37**(3), 580–607 (1994)
45. Seers, A.: Team-member exchange quality: A new construct for role-making research. Organ. Behav. Hum. Decis. Process. **43**(1), 118–135 (1989)
46. Seers, A., Petty, M.M., Cashman, J.F.: Team-member exchange under team and traditional management: A naturally occurring Quasi-Experiment. Group Organ. Manage. **20**(1), 18–38 (1995)
47. Shalley, C.E., Zhou, J., Oldham, G.R.: The effects of personal and contextual characteristics on creativity: Where should we go from here? J. Manage. **30**(6), 933–958 (2004)
48. Sosik, J.J., Godshalk, V.M.: Leadership, mentoring functions received, and job-related stress: A conceptual model and preliminary study. J. Organ. Behav. **21**(4), 365–390 (2000)
49. Sternberg, R.J.: The Nature of Creativity: Contemporary Psychological Perspectives. Cambridge University Press, Cambridge (1988)
50. Susskind, A.M., Kacmar, K.M., Borchgrevink, C.P.: Customer service providers' attitudes relating to customer service and customer satisfaction in the customer-server exchange. J. Appl. Psychol. **88**(1), 179–187 (2003)
51. Sutherland, V.J., Cooper, C.L.: Sources of work stress. In: Hurrell, J., Murphy, L.R., Sauter, S.L., Cooper, C.L. (eds.) Occupational Stress: Issues and Developments in Research, pp. 3–35. Taylor and Francis, New York (1988)
52. Syme, S.L.: Social epidemiology and the work environment. In: Johnson, J., Johansson, G. (eds.) The Psychosocial Work Environment: Work Organization, Democratization and Health, pp. 21–31. Baywood, Amityville, NY (1991)
53. Teichner, W.H., Arees, E., Reilly, R.: Noise and human performance: A psychophysiological approach. Ergonomics **6**(1), 83–97 (1963)
54. Tierney, P., Farmer, S.M., Graen, G.B.: An examination of leadership and employee creativity: The relevance of traits and relationships. Pers. Psychol. **52**(3), 591–620 (1999)
55. Woodman, R.W., Sawyer, J.E., Griffin, R.W.: Toward a theory of organizational creativity. Acad. Manage. Rev. **18**(2), 293–321 (1993)
56. Woodman, R.W., Schoenfeldt, L.F.: Individual differences in creativity: An interactionist perspective. In: Glover, J.A., Ronning, R.E., Reynolds, C.R. (eds.) Handbook of Creativity, pp. 77–92. Plenum Press, New York (1989)
57. Yerkes, R.M., Dodson, J.D.: The relation of strength of stimulus to rapidity of habit-formation. J. Comp. Neurol. Psychol. **18**(5), 459–482 (1908)
58. Zhou, J., George, J.M.: When job dissatisfaction leads to creativity: Encouraging the expression of voice. Acad. Manage. J. **44**(4), 682–696 (2001)

Chapter 2
Computer-Mediated Task Performance Under Stress and Non-stress Conditions: Emphasis on Physiological Approaches

Nam Yong Jo, Kun Chang Lee, and Dae Sung Lee

2.1 Introduction

Recently, as competition in most industries grows more fierce, the performance of tasks managed by human labor is also strongly required to be improved. These environments make an employee be more anxious for their job performance, and more demands are requested to employees giving them more time pressers. The anxiety and time pressure are distinguishing features of job related stress in the organizational field of studies. The human performance in the working environments has attracted researchers' interest for a long time. Also, psychological, organizational, and educational literatures have discussed the relationship between stress and performance with considerable attention. However, little research has focused on the performance of computer-mediated task in physiological manners. The computer-mediated task performance is worthy of our attention because most of tasks in the office workplace are performed with personal computers. Thus, considering the prior research about the relationship between stress and performance, this study suggests physiological approach to measure stress and analyze the effect of it on task performance. For the experiments, we adopted two stress manipulations, performance feedback for arising anxiety and time pressure, for stress conditions. The well-known Window's game Minesweeper is employed as a substitute for computer-mediated task; subjects are requested to play Minesweeper under controlled

N.Y. Jo • D.S. Lee
SKK Business School, Sungkyunkwan University, Seoul 110-745, Republic of Korea
e-mail: namyong.jo@gmail.com; leeds1122@gmail.com

K.C. Lee (✉)
Department of Interaction Science, SKK Business School, Sungkyunkwan University, Seoul 110-745, Republic of South Korea
e-mail: kunchanglee@gmail.com

K.C. Lee (ed.), *Digital Creativity: Individuals, Groups, and Organizations*, Integrated Series in Information Systems 32, DOI 10.1007/978-1-4614-5749-7_2, © Springer Science+Business Media New York 2013 conditions. To measure subjects' stress physiologically, galvanic skin response (GSR) and electrocardiogram (ECG) are recorded with Biopac MP100. A total of 32 employed subjects are randomly assigned two groups (e.g., stress group and non-stress group) then GSR and ECG signals are recorded during their game playing. After the experiment, the subjects are requested to complete the questionnaire using the perceived stress scale (PSS) which consisted of stress-related questions to underpin the results of physiological signals.

The remainder of the paper is organized as follows: We start with reviewing previous studies about stress, task performance and stress. In section three, the methodology adopted in this study is introduced with explanation of subjects. The statistical analysis is put in fourth. Finally, concluding remarks with implications and limitations are discussed in the last sections.

2.2   Theoretical Background

2.2.1   Stress and Task Performance

There has been controversial study about the influence of stress on performance [1–6]. Some researchers insist that stress has negative impact on the performance; other researchers insist that stress has a positive influence on the performance [7]. According to prior studies, this inconsistency seems to be rooted in two major findings. For one thing, the arousal level come from stress increase performance up to a certain threshold, but it decreases performance after reaching that point of over-arousal; thus, positive/negative stress' influence on performance is dependent on which level of arousal the stress is measuring at purposely or coincidently. For another, some researches insist there is challenge stress (i.e., the level or the demands of the work itself and workload), which is positively related to the performance, and hindrance stress (i.e., role ambiguity, role conflict, and hassles), which influence negatively on the performance. For instance, in study of [8] shows that hindrance stress is negative related to the performance, however, challenging stress promotes motivation and positively influences performance.

In this paper we apply the challenge stress in that, first, we are interested in how the stress affect positive influences the task performance to give practical implications to the leaders in an industry. Second the hindrance stresses, such as that role ambiguity and role complict, are not easy to be adopted in the controlled experiments because the manipulation of stress should control interactions among various roles of related to a subjects' role. Thus, the stresses are use manipulated as time pressure and performance feedback on a specific group during playing Minesweeper game in this paper.

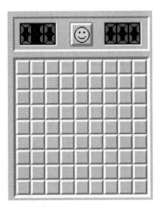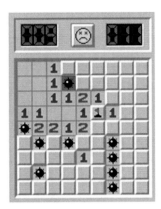

Fig. 2.1 (*Left*) The initial status of the Minesweeper. (*Right*) The last status of the Minesweeper (flag and bomb symbolize the place of bomb)

2.2.2   Minesweeper and Computer-Meditated Task

This study adopts the famous computer game for manipulating computer mediated task. The Minesweeper is a well-known Windows-based embedded game which is enjoyed by Windows users around the world. The other advantage of it is easy to learn even for a novice and the level of difficulty is controlled by the player. Thus, it has to be introduced in some researchers to discuss about algorithms of programs as well as users' behaviors in playing games [27].

In the study of [9], the Minesweeper game is introduced to explain the complexity of multi-relational learning task. Minesweeper has two major aspects to describe user's task performance. First, one realizes the complexity of the game by calculating an estimate for the size of its search space. In the given 9×9 board with $M = 10$ mines (see Fig. 2.1) at the beginning of the game, the player has 81 tiles from which to uncover tile; moreover, there are situations that can be "solved" with nontrivial reasoning in the process of playing the game. For example, considering Fig. 2.1 left where the only available information about the board states is the numbers. After careful analysis, one finds that the squares with containing a mine (see Fig. 2.1 right) and no mine, the square with a flag is a mine, and the state of the blank tiles cannot be determined until we know how many mines are hidden in the board. There are other Minesweeper situations where the available information is not enough to identify a safe square or a mine, as in Fig. 2.2, and the best option available to the player is to make an informed guess (i.e., a guess that minimizes the risk of being blown up by uncovering a mine).

In this work, we consider playing Minesweeper is closer to performing the task in the working environments in that player are first supposed to find the problem (i.e., realize the complexity of the game), then recognize that problem and choose alternatives to solve the problems (i.e., uncovering the tile), which are the typical

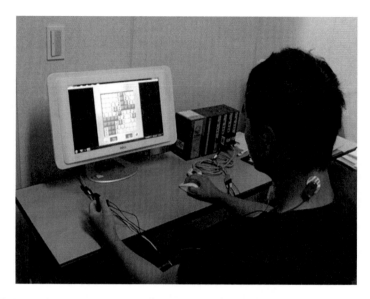

Fig. 2.2 Measuring physiological sign during playing Minesweeper

processes of humans in performing their work; moreover, all of this work is mediated by personal computer.

2.2.3   Assessment of the Stress

In this research, the stress is measured psychologically as well as physiologically. Psychological measures are dominantly used in the organization fields of studies, physiological measures are typically adopted in the fields of physiological psychology frequently. We mainly focus on the physiological measures, because they are the only method to measure real-time stress of subjects in performing their tasks, which makes this study differentiate from prior researches. Brief introductions of both of the assessments are as follows.

2.2.3.1   Psychological Assessment

Stress response can be measured and evaluated in terms of perceptual, behavioral, and physical responses. The evaluation of perceptual responses to a stressor involves subjective estimations and perceptions. Self-reported questionnaires have been the most common instruments used in measuring stress [10]. There are well-know representative measures such as PSS [11], the Life Events and Coping Inventory (LECI) [16], and the Stress Response Inventory (SRI) [12].

The physical response to stress has two components: a physiological response indicative of central-autonomic activity and a biochemical response involving

Table 2.1 Stress manipulation stimuli

Question	Ref.
In this experiment, how have you been upset because of something that happened unexpectedly?	[11]
In this experiment, how have you felt that you were unable to control the important things?	
In this experiment, how have you felt nervous and stressed?	
In this experiment, how have you felt confident about your ability to handle your personal problems? (Reverse)	
In this experiment, how have you felt that things were going your way? (Reverse)	
In this experiment, how have you found that you could not cope with all the things that you had to do?	
In this experiment, how have you been able to control irritations? (Reverse)	
In this experiment, how have you felt that you were on top of things? (Reverse)	
In this experiment, how have you been angered because of things that were outside of your control?	
In this experiment, how have you felt difficulties were piling up so high that you could not overcome them	

changes in the endocrine and immune systems [13]. PSS is adopted in thin study because it is very common in the prior research about stress. Table 2.1 shows the description of the questionnaire.

2.2.3.2 Physiological Assessment

Stress induces a change in autonomic physiological functioning [14]. Stress also has an impact on blood pressure and heart rate, which is reflecting a predominance of sympathetic nervous system (SNS) activity [15]. Heart rate variability (HRV) is beat-to-beat variation in heart rate, and it has been used as a biomarker of autonomic nervous system (ANS) activity associated with stress [16]. HRV analysis is generally divided into two categories: time-domain and frequency-domain methods. Time-domain analysis of HRV involves quantifying the mean or standard deviation of RR intervals (SDNN). In the one hand, frequency-domain analysis involves calculating the power of the respiratory-dependent high frequency (HF) and low frequency (LF) components of HRV. For our experiment, we select the standard deviation of RR intervals and LF/HF ratio as ECG information. Stress has been reported to evoke a decrease in the high-frequency component and an increase in the low-frequency component of HRV [17]. Therefore, LF/HF ratio is supposed to increases if stress arises. On the other hand, a decrease of SDNN is reported to be related to an increased level of stress. In addition, GSR is a measure of the electrical resistance of the skin. A transient increase in skin conductance is proportional to sweat secretion [18]. Thus, whenever an individual is getting stress, sweat-gland activity is activated and increases skin conductance. Since the sweat glands are also controlled by the SNS, skin conductance works as an indicator for sympathetic activation due to the stress reaction.

2.3   Method

2.3.1   Participants

Thirty-seven healthy subjects participated in this experiment from undergraduate students at a Korean university whose saw the post of Internet bulletin board. Prior to the experiment, the subjects were given written and verbal information explaining the experimental procedures. We confirmed through interviews that none of the subjects used medication for hypertension or any other cardiovascular disease and they were all free of any nervous or other psychological disorder. We received written informed consent from all participants and each subject was paid 20,000 Korean won for reward of participation. Among them, six subjects with corrupted data were eliminated from this study, then finally total of 32 subjects were employed for the tests (see Table 2.2). The mean age was 22 years (range of 18–26 years). Some of the subjects were randomly assigned to stress manipulations. Consequently, the subjects were divided into two groups (stress group, $n = 16$; non-stress group, $n = 16$).

2.3.2   Experimental Procedure

Before the experiment, the subjects were asked to know and show how to play the game Minesweeper. In the event subjects were unfamiliar with the game, they were instructed how to play the game and, under research assistant guidance, to practice it over 20 min until they were accustomed to play. Then, they were requested to cleanse their hands and remove all accessories from their body before measurement to avoid noises of recoding physiological signs. Then, the subjects were directed to sit comfortably and keep their left hand motionlessly when the experiment started.

Table 2.2 Stress manipulation stimuli

AGE	Non-stress group		Stress group	
	Female	Male	Female	Male
19	2	2	1	
20	2	2	1	2
21	1	1	1	
22				1
23		1		2
24	1	1		5
25		2		3
26		1		
Total	6	10	3	13

Each subject was asked to attach two GSR electrodes to the index and middle finger of the left hand and place three ECG electrodes on their chest and abdomen. This experiment used a Biopac MP100 series for the measuring and an AcqKnowledge 4.1 for the analysis. After GSR and ECG signals had showed normal waves, the subjects were instructed to start mediating for 7 min in order to acquire baseline data from GSR and ECG signals. And then they played the Minesweeper in 7 min. They could play as many games as they could finish during the given time, regardless of their win or loss of game play. In the course of playing, GSR and ECG signals were measured for both the stress and non-stress group. Their computer-mediated performances were recorded in the form of number of winning or losing games and time spend for those. After finishing the game and their physiological signs were recorded, the subjects were requested to complete the questionnaire survey, which consisted of stress items. Figure 2.2. represents the circumstance of subjects and physiology signal recording when playing the Minesweeper.

2.3.2.1 Performance of Task

The performance measure of playing Minesweeper was also suggested in [9]. In that research the performance is measured with the accuracy of sweeping numbers of mines rather than sweeping speed. In the study of [19], the number of correctly-placed flags-per-second (Pmines) is counted. In our experiments, both measures of prior researches are adopted after manipulation to evaluate the performance of task. For the purpose, we normalize both the number of wins of games, which is the perfect sweeping of the mines, and the average time of the game. Then both variables are integrated into one variable by Principal Component Analysis (PCA) to make a performance index of for the test (see Table 2.4).

2.3.2.2 Stress Manipulation

Four types of stress manipulations (e.g., competition, performance feedback, reward, and time pressure) were used on the subjects of the stress group. The performance feedback under stress manipulations has been also used by [20] study. During the experiments, the subjects were informed and stimulated every 30 s with verbal comments by an assistant. Every comment is typically manipulated to stimulate subjects' stress of anxiety or stress of time pressure. For example, after 30 s they start to play the assistant say, "The best recode of previous tries of subject was 11 s. for a game" then another 30 s later the assistant gave them a comment of, "Try to play better!" to stimulate their anxiety of competition. Again, they are told, "If you can't complete more than ten games you get only half of the expected reward," and "Speed up!" to give them time pressure. These manipulations were implemented according to a fixed pattern, independent of actual performance. The effectiveness of these comments to create stress conditions are verified by analyzes records of physiological signals and questionnaire survey. Table 2.3 describes comments of stimuli used in the experiments.

Table 2.3 Stress manipulation stimuli

Types	Stimuli	Interval	Repetitions
Competition	The best recode of previous tries of subject was 11 s for a game	30 s	3
	I can do better than you	2 min 30 s	
	Female/male student do play better	4 min 30 s	
Performance feedback	Try to play better!	1 min	4
	You are no better than expected!	3 min	
	You can do better!	5 min	
Reward	If you cannot complete more than ten games you get only half of the expected reward	1 min 30 s	3
	If you break new record, you be paid extra reward	3 min 30 s	
	It seems you may come tomorrow and do the play again	5 min	
Time pressure	Speed up!	2 min	N/A
	You have 3 min	4 min	
	Try to complete one game in 30 s	6 min	

2.3.2.3 Questionnaire Survey

In order to compare physiological signals under manipulated stress with perceived stress of individuals, we conducted questionnaire survey, which has been more familiar method to measure level of stress in the organizational field of researches. The degree of stress given to the subjects can be measured with more confidence. In other words, by observing the stress from view of different angle, we can improve the accuracy of measures and be more confident. This kind of measure is called *Triangulation* of measures. For this study, we adopt PSS for survey items [10, 11]. The PSS measures the degree to which situations are considered stressful by addressing events experienced beforehand. It is designed to quantify how unpredictable, uncontrollable, and overloaded adults find their lives. We conducted another survey to see whether or not self-reported creativity [21, 22] would agree with actual creative performance. Each item in our survey was measured on a seven-point Likert scale, with answers ranging from "strongly disagree" to "strongly agree." The items in the survey were developed by adopting existing measures validated by other researchers Table 2.4.

2.3.3 Statistics

For physiological signals and task performance assessment, the differences between the stress group and the non-stress group are analyzed with the Mann–Whitney *U* Test.

Table 2.4 Physiological signals and task performance of subjects

Conditions	Signals			Performance of win		
	GSR	STD RR	LF/HF	Repetitions	Sum of sec.	Average
(a) Under non-stress condition						
Non-stress	0.084	0.107	−0.422	5	113	22.60
	0.109	−0.125	0.468	2	174	87.00
	−0.228	0.688	0.324	2	146	73.00
	−0.050	0.063	−0.287	6	150	25.00
	−0.149	0.170	0.281	2	213	106.50
	−0.168	0.705	−0.379	7	247	35.29
	−0.332	0.205	0.939	7	258	36.86
	−0.178	0.069	1.763	4	194	48.50
	0.040	0.343	−0.569	9	256	28.44
	0.252	0.036	−0.138	14	238	17.00
	0.124	0.263	0.744	2	58	29.00
	−0.228	1.311	0.169	0	0	0.00
	−0.069	−0.204	−0.693	4	235	58.75
	−0.139	0.330	0.018	1	76	76.00
	−0.342	3.084	−0.078	1	161	161.00
	0.559	0.493	−0.403	0	0	0.00
(b) Under stress condition						
Stress	0.208	−0.159	−0.742	2	183	91.50
	0.104	0.288	−0.153	4	169	42.25
	0.035	−0.266	0.125	6	267	44.50
	−0.020	0.359	0.472	8	122	15.25
	0.297	−0.209	2.085	0	0	0.00
	0.332	1.072	2.179	2	89	44.50
	−0.173	0.160	0.530	1	42	42.00
	−0.480	0.265	1.372	0	0	0.00
	−0.307	0.009	1.927	8	238	29.75
	−0.020	0.065	2.646	0	0	0.00
	−0.094	−0.111	−0.225	0	0	0.00
	0.010	−0.126	−0.143	7	153	21.86
	−0.079	0.391	0.266	1	114	114.00
	−0.025	1.082	1.581	0	0	0.00
	0.030	−0.296	0.047	4	193	48.25
	−0.287	0.059	3.921	2	207	103.50

Notice: all values in the table are normalized

Mann–Whitney U Test is one of the most well-known and nonparametric significance tests. It is a nonparametric statistical test to see if one of two samples of independent observations tends to have larger values than the other out of small samples. Thus, it is suitable for the analysis because, we have only 32 subjects who participated independently in the study. In our test, the null hypothesis is the computer-mediated task performance of the stress group is not different from that of the non-stress group. The results from the Mann–Whitney U Test are presented with the p-value; thus, statistical significance was assumed for p-value <0.05 under 99.5% confidence level in our test.

Then, we investigated the performance ratings for each group with the Wilcoxon signed ranks test. Finally, we examined the differences between the computer mediated job performance of stress group and that of non-stress group through descriptive statistics.

2.4   Results

2.4.1   Differences Between Stress Group and Non-stress Group

2.4.1.1   Physiological Signals and Self-Reported Stress

The relationship between manipulated stress and physiological signals (Normalized ΔGSR, ΔSDNN, and ΔLF/HF ratio) are investigated using the Mann–Whitney U Test. This test is one of the most powerful nonparametric tests, and it is a most useful alternative to the parametric test when the researcher wishes to avoid the test's assumptions or when the sample sizes are relatively small [23]. The results of physiological signals show that there are no significant difference between the stress and non-stress groups for normalized ΔGSR (p-value$=0.62>0.05$) and ΔSDNN (p-value$=0.12>0.05$). We confirmed that the stress group had a higher ΔLF/HF (p-value$=0.04<0.05$) ratio value than the non-stress group, with statistical significance (see Table 2.5).

As is discussed in the prior paragraph, questionnaire survey (PSS) is also conducted to compare subjects in stress group with them of non-stress group. Statistically significant differences between the two groups are also analyzed by the Mann–Whitney U Test. The result shows that the cognitive stress of the stress group is significantly higher than the other (p-value<0.01). Thus, we assure that our manipulation of stress conditions has been well controlled in the experiment and we can be sure to discriminate the stress group from the other. In other words, although we could not verify the difference between the two groups for task performance through the Mann–Whitney U Test, we made sure that the stress group has more perceived stress than the non-stress group.

2.4.1.2   Task Performance Assessment

To measure computer-mediated task performance, the number of wins out of all iteration of playing and the averaged duration time of them are considered at the same time. Not only doing things correctly but also doing it productively is considered as a performance in a real working environment. Thus, both factors are integrated to make index of performance using PCA. Then, Mann–Whitney U Test is applied also for analysis of the differences between the two groups. The result shows no significant difference between the performances of task of the stress group and the other (see Table 2.6).

Table 2.5 Mann–Whitney U test results for physiological signals and task performance

Group	N	Normalized ΔGSR Mean	SD	Normalized ΔSDNN Mean	SD	Normalized ΔLF/HF ratio Mean	SD	Self-reported stress Mean	SD
Stress	16	−0.029	0.215	0.161	0.418	0.993	1.292	4.475	1.012
Non-stress	16	−0.045	0.234	0.471	0.789	0.109	0.642	3.213	1.018
Total	32	−0.037	0.221	0.316	0.641	0.551	1.099	3.844	1.187
Two-tailed probability		0.624		0.122		**0.042***		**0.007****	

*Statistically significant at $p < 0.05$
**Statistically significant at p < 0.01

Table 2.6 Mann–Whitney U test results for physiological signals and self-reported stress

Group	N	Performance Mean	SD
Stress	16	0.308	1.741
Non-stress	16	−0.352	1.798
Total	32	−0.022	1.773
Two-tailed probability		0.344	

*Statistically significant at $p < 0.05$
**Statistically significant at $p < 0.01$

2.5   Discussion

There has been consistent research regarding the effect of stress on task performance, but the prior studies have not reached on the agreement of majority in terms of relationship. Some of the researches insist that stress positively affects task performance; however, other researches are arguing opposite results even curvilinear relationship [24, 25]. Those contradictable results, sometimes, come from focusing on different type of stress (e.g., challenging stress and hindrance stress) or level of difficulties of the tasks. Moreover, most of studies about challenging stress have analyzed subjects' cognitive level of stress but physiological approaches have not tried abundant. In this research, the direct relationship between real-time challenging stress and performance of computer mediated task is discussed.

For differentiated approach, we adapt physiological measures to examine the direct relationship between stress and the performance of computer mediated task. For the purpose, we employed 32 volunteered students randomly and then placed them under the manipulated stress condition that mainly consists of task anxiety and time pressure. They were separated into two groups that are stress group and non-stress group. Under the manipulated conditions they were required to play Minesweeper which is assumed to be operationally common to computer mediated task. During playing games their physiological signals were recorded as an index of real-time stress, then they have been analyzed to see if there are statistically different degrees of stress between two groups. The result of analysis of ΔLF/HF ratio and questionnaire survey shows their stress level of each group is significantly different physiologically and cognitively. Nevertheless, their analyzed performances showed that they are not significantly different from each other; thus, we carefully assume that the real-time stress level does not significantly affect the level of performance.

To conclude, our major implications and findings are follows. First, although we measured three kinds of physiological signals that are reported to be useful signals (e.g., GSR, SDNN, and LF/HF) for tracing stress level, only LF/HF shows significant difference between the stress group and non-stress group. That means the frequency-domain method, which is calculating the power of respiratory, is the better choice. In other words, for the manipulated conditions characterizing real-time and short period (e.g., 7 min in this study), LF/HF is effective signals to analyze. Second, the real-time stress conditions do not influence computer-mediated tasks in this study. Stress and performance has not been consistent in the prior research; rather than concluding the results as pointless, we can suggest further possibilities of stress' affect on task performance if it is combined with various factors, for example, the skills and knowledge for doing specific tasks.

Some limitations are worth attention for the future research. We suggest two main design issues on the stress–performance experiments. First, the characters of subjects should be considered because it is not clear if they are encouraged to challenge under manipulated challenging stress. Depending on subjects' personality, they are neither anxious nor easy to feel timely pressure. Second, as is in prior researches, mediating variables should be sufficiently considered. For example, relationships between stress and motivation have not been studied much, nor has an agreement been reached in the existing theories [26], so they can chose topic of motivation and stress. Finally, the performance deviation can be aroused by skill, rather than stress condition, which means although challenge stress is motivational and promoting performance, the influence of skill cannot be effectively detected. We suggest these findings should be strictly controlled in future research.

Acknowledgments This work was supported by the Korea Research Foundation Grant funded by the Korean Government (KRF-2009-342-B00015). This study was also partially supported by WCU (World Class University) program through the National Research Foundation of Korea funded by the Ministry of Education, Science and Technology (Grant No. R31-2008-000-10062-0).

References

1. Abramis, D.J.: Work role ambiguity, job satisfaction, and job performance: Meta-analysis and review. Psychol. Rep. **75**, 1411–1433 (1994)
2. Hockey, R., Hamilton, P.: The cognitive patterning of stress. In: Hockey, R. (ed.) Stress and Fatigue in Human, pp. 331–362. Wiley, Chichester, England (1983)
3. Jackson, S.E., Schuler, R.S.: A meta-analysis and conceptual critique of research on role ambiguity and role conflict in work settings. Organ. Behav. Hum. Decis. Process. **36**, 16–78 (1985)
4. Kahn, R.L., Byosiere, P.: Stress in organizations. In: Dunnette, M.D., Hough, L.M. (eds.) Handbook of Industrial and Organizational Psychology, 2nd ed, vol. 3, 571–650. Consulting Psychologists Press, Palo Alto, CA (1992)

5. McGrath, J.E., McGrath, J.E.: Stress and behavior in organizations. In: Dunnette, M.D. (ed.) Handbook of Industrial and Organizational Psychology, pp. 1351–1395. Rand McNally, Chicago (1976)
6. Spector, P.E., Dwyer, D.J., Jex, S.M.: Relation of job stressors to affective, health, and performance outcomes: A comparison of multiple data sources. J. Appl. Psychol. **73**, 11–19 (1988)
7. Fay, D., Sonnentag, S.: Rethinking the effects of stressors: A longitudinal study on personal initiative. J. Occup. Health Psychol. **7**, 221–234 (2002)
8. LePine, J.A., Podsakoff, N.P., LePine, M.A.: A meta-analytic test of the challenge stressor-hindrance stressor framework: An explanation for inconsistent relationships among stressors and performance. Acad. Manage. J. **48**, 764–775 (2005)
9. Castillo, L., Wrobel, S.: Learning minesweeper with multirelational learning. Proceedings of the 18th International Joint Conference on Artificial Intelligence, pp. 533–538 (2003)
10. Cohen, S., Williamson, G.: Perceived stress in a probability sample of the United States. In: Spacapan, S., Oskamp, S. (eds.) The Social Psychology of Health. Sage, Newbury Park, CA (1988)
11. Cohen, S., Kamarck, T., Mermelstein, R.: A global measure of perceived stress. J. Health Soc. Behav. **24**, 386–396 (1983)
12. Koh, K., Park, J., Kim, C., Cho, S.: Development of the stress response inventory and its application in clinical practice. Psychosom. Med. **63**, 668–678 (2001)
13. Cohen, S., Kessler, R., Gordon, L.: Measuring Stress—A Guide for Health and Social Scientists. Oxford University Press, New York (1997)
14. Van der Kar, L.D., Blair, M.L.: Forebrain pathways mediating stress induced hormone secretion. Front. Neuroendocrinol. **20**, 41–48 (1999)
15. Ritvanen, T., Louhevaara, V., Helin, P., Vaisanen, S., Hanninen, O.: Responses of the autonomic nervous system during periods of perceived high and low work stress in younger and older female teachers. Appl. Ergon. **37**, 311–318 (2005)
16. Zhong, X., Hilton, H.J., Gates, G.J., Jelic, S., Stern, Y., Bartels, M.N., DeMeersman, R.E., Basner, R.C.: Increased sympathetic and decreased parasympathetic cardiovascular modulation in normal humans with acute sleep deprivation. J. Appl. Physiol. **98**, 2024–2032 (2005)
17. Bernardi, L., Wdowczyk-Szulc, J., Valenti, C., Castoldi, S., Passino, C., Spadacini, G., Sleight, P.: Effects of controlled breathing, mental activity, and mental stress with or without verbalization on heart rate variability. J. Am. Coll. Cardiol. **35**, 1462–1469 (2000)
18. Darrow, C.: The rationale for treating the change in galvanic skin response as a change in conductance. Psychophysiology **1**, 31–38 (1964)
19. Ivanov, S.V.: Theoretical and experimental models in physiological and psychological research of pattern perception and recognition in humans. Pattern Recogn. Image Anal. **19**, 114–122 (2009)
20. Bogdan, R., Pizzagalli, D.A.: Acute stress reduces reward responsiveness: Implications for depression. Biol. Psychiatry **60**, 1147–1154 (2006)
21. Oldham, G.R., Cummings, A.: Employee creativity: Personal and contextual factors at work. Acad. Manage. J. **39**, 607–634 (1996)
22. Shalley, C.E., Gilson, L.L., Blum, T.C.: Interactive effects of growth need strength, self-reported creative performance. Acad. Manage. J. **52**, 489–505 (2009)
23. Siegel, S., Castellan, N.J.: Nonparametric Statistics for the Behavioural Sciences. McGraw-Hill, New York (1988)
24. Jamal, M.: Job stress and job performance controversy, An empirical assessment. Organ. Behav. Hum. Perform. **33**, 1–21 (1984)
25. Jamal, M.: Relationship of job stress to job performance: A study of managers and blue-collar workers. Hum. Relat. **38**, 409–424 (1985)
26. Perrewe, P.L., Zellars, K.L.: An examination of attributions and emotions in the transactional approach to the organizational stress process. J. Organ. Behav. **20**, 739–152 (1999)
27. Kaye, R.: Minesweeper is NP-complete. Math. Intel. **22**, 9–15 (2000)

Chapter 3
Pattern Analysis of the Creativity of a Digitalist Considering Its Antecedents and Task Diversity: A Multi-Agent Simulation Approach

Young Wook Seo, Kun Chang Lee, and Seong Wook Chae

3.1 Introduction

We are now living in a digital age, and the digitalization of societal aspects has many effects ranging from the work environment to one's personal life. Digitalization is an indicator that our work and personal lives are heavily dependent on different types of digital devices, with the benefit of easily and effectively performing specific processes. Social networking Web sites such as Facebook, Twitter, and Cyworld have recently emerged as essential communication vehicles and are examples of recent trends in digitalization. In the current period of transition toward a digital society, the methods firms use to remain competitive in the marketplace have changed significantly. In the past, production efficiency with low cost and high quality was the only viable (and best) option for most companies. There is little doubt that this approach is still effective today. However, the weight traditionally assigned to production efficiency has diminished significantly. Knowledge-driven competitiveness has instead emerged as a new way to improve a company's sustainable competitiveness [10, 49]. The problem at hand is how a company achieves this so-called knowledge-driven competitiveness. In the literature, creativity is a good source for establishing knowledge-driven competitiveness and making a significant

Y.W. Seo
Software Engineering Center at NIPA, Seoul 138-711, Republic of Korea
e-mail: seoyy123@gmail.com

K.C. Lee (✉)
Department of Interaction Science, SKK Business School, Sungkyunkwan University,
Seoul 110-745, Republic of South Korea
e-mail: kunchanglee@gmail.com

S.W. Chae
SKK Business School, Management Research Institute, Sungkyunkwan University,
Seoul 110-745, Republic of Korea
e-mail: seongwookchae@gmail.com

K.C. Lee (ed.), *Digital Creativity: Individuals, Groups, and Organizations*,
Integrated Series in Information Systems 32, DOI 10.1007/978-1-4614-5749-7_3,
© Springer Science+Business Media New York 2013

impact in the market. One of the advantages of creativity is that its cost of production is almost zero. Furthermore, once products and services that are recognized by customers as "creative" are released to the market, the company's anticipated market share is nearly monopolized. Such a scenario prevents potential rival companies from entering the market and competing with the innovating firm.

The importance of enhancing the value-added nature of products and services by utilizing the principle of creativity has recently gained attention from both academics and practitioners. The concept of creativity is not new in the field of management studies [46, 51], and various works, including scholarly journal publications and mass-media articles, have stressed the importance of creativity in market competition. However, researchers are quite concerned with the absence of a sound mechanism through which creativity can be applied to companies across various industries. The concept of creativity is almost abused in today's world, and there are still many problems that researchers must address, including the following: (1) how to redefine creativity in a digital society, (2) how to identify the antecedents of digital creativity so that it can be seamlessly materialized in the working environment, and (3) how to analyze the influence of task diversity on digital creativity in order to motivate companies to adopt digital creativity as an important strategic initiative. The main objective of this study is to address and resolve the aforementioned issues related to the concept of creativity.

3.2   Theoretical Background

3.2.1   Creativity

Creativity is a concept used in many fields in various ways. Though researchers have offered a variety of definitions, creativity can be defined as the ability to produce work that is both novel and useful [1, 32, 45]. Creativity has generally been studied from one of two contexts: the personal context and the organizational context.

3.2.1.1   Creativity in the Personal Context

From a personal context, creativity can be explored through the use of pluralistic and professional field approaches. The pluralistic approach to creativity research was developed to resolve problems derived from the narrow-minded analysis of the single-academic approach. This approach hypothesizes that creativity is generated based on a combination of various elements [12, 34, 44, 53] and focuses on the changes in, and interaction of, personal characteristics and the elements surrounding individuals. Sternberg and Lubart [44] suggested "the nature of creativity," where creativity can be explained through a combination of six factors: intelligence, knowledge, thinking styles, personality, motivation, and the environmental context. All of these factors must be considered in creativity research.

In another approach to personal creativity, Mansfield and Busse [33] divided creativity into amateur creativity and professional creativity based on the level of the resulting products. The researchers used "auctorive" to explain professional creativity and suggested dividing a portion of creativity into the auctorive creativity of professionals in specific fields and the amateur creativity of normal people.

3.2.1.2   Creativity in an Organizational Context

In this study, creativity in an organizational context is divided into organizational creativity and creativity management. Creativity is a process, so we must consider it a learnable trait [31]. In other words, both personal and organizational characteristics should be developed and managed to lead to the desired level of creativity. Ricchiuto [39] stated that creativity has various functions including the improvement of an organization, problem-solving, and the resolution of conflicts. In addition, the need for multidimensional research on individuals, groups, and the creativity of an organization has recently been suggested. Meanwhile, team creativity depends on the nature of interactions among team members and the social environment. Therefore, team creativity is also influenced by the factors representing organizational features, such as group learning, group diversity, network structure, project types, and so on [9, 16, 27].

Creativity management is a crucial topic to consider in the debate about the innovative research department [4]. Creativity management is defined as the management of facilitators and barriers in order to create new ideas and achieve successful results from a macroscopic perspective, including individuals and organizations [2, 4]. The concept of creativity management is generally formed through diversity, autonomy, redundancy, connectivity, and flexibility.

3.2.2   Digital Creativity and Digitalists

Saunders and Gero [40] presented a novel approach to the computational study of creativity, called artificial creativity, which promotes the study of the creative behavior of individuals and societies in the artificial societies of agents [40]. Digital creativity is assumed in the present study to be applied in the individual and professional fields, and in this context, the term individual refers only to the digitalist members of society, or people who think and act digitally. Such people comprise a major portion of the current knowledge-based society. Digital creativity is not just a simple technology; it is "an ability to resolve problems as well as create new and useful products when dealing with tasks in the digital environment." A digitalist is defined in the present study not as a comprehensive concept but as a knowledge worker who deals with given tasks efficiently and creatively in the digital environments of actual companies. In the analysis of the relationships between digital creativity and evolution, it has been emphasized that in order to support open-ended and creative evolution, it is fundamental for digitalists to be part of the environment experienced by other digitalists [14, 47].

3.2.3 Team and Task Diversity

Along with greater interdependence and larger portions of work likely to be done in small teams, heterogeneity — or diversity — marks the experience of work [19]. Team diversity may be divided into two categories: surface-level diversity and deep-level diversity. Surface-level diversity is defined as differences among team members in overt demographic characteristics [20, 21]. These characteristics, including age, sex, and race/ethnicity, are often reflected in physical features. Surface-level diversity is equivalent to what other researchers have labeled "social category diversity" [25] or "demographic diversity" [36].

Deep-level diversity refers to differences among team members' psychological characteristics, including personalities, values, and attitudes [20, 21]. Clues to these latent individual differences are taken from members' interactions with one another as they unfold over time. Those clues are expressed in behavior patterns, verbal and nonverbal communication, and exchanges of personal information [21]. At the individual level, Barrick and Mount [5] demonstrated that conscientiousness was the "Big Five" personality dimension most consistently and most strongly related to performance in a variety of task settings. However, Barrick et al. [6] found mixed effects of conscientiousness at the team level, reporting that higher mean levels of team conscientiousness were associated with team performance but that team member diversity in conscientiousness was not associated with team viability or social cohesion [20].

As time passes, increasing collaboration weakens the effects of surface-level (demographic) diversity on team outcomes but strengthens those of deep-level (psychological) diversity [21]. Perceived diversity transmits the impact of actual diversity on a team's social integration, which in turn affects task performance [21].

To reach organizational goals, organizations attract members, form structures and systems, and create products, services, or knowledge to be delivered at particular points in time [19]. Because of the complexity involved in creating such high-quality and timely deliverables, differentiation of individual roles within the organization's structures and systems is necessary [19]. Such role differentiation is also manifested, with both jobs and tasks varying in organizations.

3.2.4 Multi-Agent Simulation

An intelligent agent (or simply "agent") is a computer system that is capable of flexible autonomous action in dynamic, unpredictable, and (typically) multi-agent domains, though it has various definitions because of the multiple roles it can perform [23, 38]. To address the need to use MAS to investigate team creativity from the knowledge-network perspective, let us consider the notion of emergence, which is one of the most important ideas to come from complexity theory [43, 50]. Complexity theory tells us that emergence is not observable by analyzing the actions or behaviors of individual agents. In this sense, emergence is a collective behavior, or macro-behavior [42]. In social science-related topics, MAS provides only one viable option for simulating emergence, based on a specific set of conditions in which each individual agent is assumed to behave in a very simple way [15].

Palmer [37] conducted simulations of category elaboration using a multi-agent system in order to measure the diversity and performance of a test group. When performing a social simulation of micro/macro issues in the electronic market, Hahn et al. [17] used multi-agent technology to research social reputations through flexible, self-regulated mechanisms. As mentioned above, a great deal of research on MASs related to organization and performance has been conducted in the social sciences.

3.3 Research Model

In this paper, creativity is defined as "an ability to create something new and valuable and is determined by interactions among personal affective tendency, cognitive ability, environment, and task." Accordingly, a conceptual model of creativity is suggested to explain the relationships among these factors. Constructs and relationships suitable for digital creativity were also reconstructed, and a research model of digital creativity was generated. The proposed research model to be used for MAS is shown in Fig. 3.1.

Extensive research has shown the effects of the surrounding environment, such as culture and climate, on the creativity of individuals [48, 52]. Contexts and social influences related to creative activities include the physical environment, culture, group or organization's "climate," restrictions due to time/work, expectations, compensation/punishment, and role models. Generally, these factors are elements of the environmental and social background of creative activities [53]. In this digital age, organizations have an interest in whether communication effectiveness among employees influences creativity and performance in the digital environment.

Canessa and Riolo [8] suggested that the degree of stability in the contact networks affecting organizational culture strength is closely related to communication effectiveness, which in turn influences organizational performance. Canessa and Riolo [8] defined and used communication effectiveness (CE) as a function based on the difference in culture between two agents:

$$CE_{jk} = \frac{1}{1 + e^{\left(\sum_{i=1}^{N} |Tij - Tik|\right)\alpha - \beta}} \tag{3.1}$$

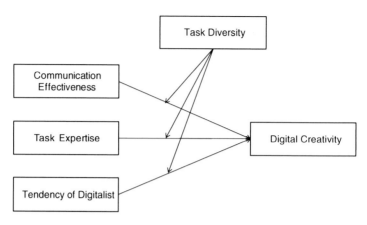

Fig. 3.1 Research model

where Tij is the ith dimension of the culture of agent "j", Tik is the ith dimension of the culture of agent "k", and N is the number of cultural dimensions. The constants α and β are used to adjust the shape of the sigmoid curve.

Creative thinking and production are influenced by the level of an individual's expertise and proficiency in a specific field [13, 44]. Therefore, task expertise has a positive influence on digital creativity. Researchers have explored personalities related to creative activities from various perspectives, including the following: (1) personality theory, which explains creativity within a comprehensive personality; (2) characteristics of creative activities and autobiographical features of extremely creative people in various fields; and (3) an examination of the relationship between "characteristics of personality" and creative activities [34, 53]. Therefore, the tendencies of a digitalist have a positive influence on digital creativity.

Based on social network theory, Ashworth and Carley [3] defined the following formula for the task exclusivity index (TEI) from the existing concept defined by Brass [7], Hinings et al. [22], and Dubin [11]. This formula was investigated in the current study for its influence on team performance.

$$\text{TEI}_n = \frac{1}{\text{TEI}^{\max}} \sum_{t=1}^{\hat{t}} \alpha_t T_{Nnt} e^{(1 - \bar{T}_{Nt})} \tag{3.2}$$

where $\bar{T}_{Nt} = \sum_{n=1}^{\hat{n}} \frac{1}{\beta_n} T_{Nnt}$ and $\text{TEI}^{\max}$ is the largest observed value of TEI_i. Parameters α_t and β_n are weighting factors for each task t and individual n, respectively, where $\alpha_t > 0, 0 < \beta_n < 1$.

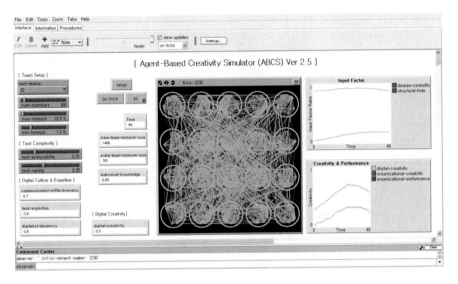

Fig. 3.2 Agent-based creativity simulator (ABCS)

3.4   Experiments

3.4.1   Platform

To test the proposed research model, a multi-agent simulator was developed to test many possible cases through simulation. In other words, in order to conduct simulation experiments, we designed an agent-based creativity simulator (ABCS) using NetLogo 4.1.2 (available at http://ccl.northwestern.edu/netlogo) (Fig. 3.2).

The ABCS used in this research model measured the attributes of each agent in order to express digital creativity at the organizational level. In other words, it collected information at the agent level and the analysis unit was the organization.

The simulation environment and assumptions are as follows. First, we designed 20 teams within an organization with a total of 300 members. Each member was assigned to one of 20 teams, and each team had a different number of members. In the simulator, communication effectiveness was applied to Formula (3.1) to recognize cultural strength as the density of the network that communicates with agents according to the social network theory. For task diversity, Formula (3.2) was applied. In addition, for task expertise, the grade of the agent was divided into high, middle, and low, and each agent was given a random value from 0 to 1 according to its grade. For tendencies of the digitalist (ToD), we defined the formula as follows:

$$ToD = \frac{(\text{originative thinking} + \text{enthusiasm})}{2}, \tag{3.3}$$

where originative thinking and enthusiasm take a random value from 0 to 1. We also defined digital creativity ($K_i(t)$) as a function of the activation level of efforts ($e_i(t)$), cumulative knowledge within teams (μ_i), and interaction among members and teams (ξ_i) based on the functions developed by Lazaric and Raybaut [29]:

$$\text{Digital Creativity} = K_i(t) = \lambda_i e_i(t), \lambda_i \mu_i + \xi_i. \tag{3.4}$$

3.4.2 Experiment Results

A total of 200 simulations were conducted from time-lag 1 to time-lag 48. Figure 3.3 shows the pattern for the average value of digital creativity over time regarding task diversity, communication effectiveness, task expertise, and tendencies of the digitalist.

The results in Fig. 3.3 show that digital creativity gradually increases over time. However, digital creativity tends to gradually decrease after a certain time-lag. These results correspond with previous research on the inverted U-shaped curve.

The pattern shown in Fig. 3.3a is as follows: In early time-lags, teams with low task diversity and high communication effectiveness (LTD-HCE) have lower levels of digital creativity than those with high task diversity and low communication effectiveness (HTD-LCE). However, in the long term, teams with high communication effectiveness (HTD-HCE, LTD-HCE) have higher levels of digital creativity than those with low communication effectiveness (HTD-LCE, LTD-LCE). Therefore, we can infer that, although task diversity is a significant factor for digital creativity, communication effectiveness can be a more significant factor in the long term. In the early part of the simulation, task diversity greatly influences digital creativity. However, as time passes, the agent affected by the digital environment exchanges the knowledge and information related to digital creativity through the network. In particular, each agent continuously explores new knowledge and information while exploiting the knowledge and information related to the task domain and creativity. As the individual agents exchange knowledge and information that are helpful in creative activities, the effectiveness of communication among the agents increases and thus the digital creativity is elevated.

Figure 3.3b, c show that high task diversity is greater for digital creativity than for low task diversity in general. Additionally, digital creativity is higher with high task expertise and high tendencies of digitalists as compared with low task expertise and low tendencies of digitalists. In other words, as time passes (time-lags 1–48), the digital creativity rank of HTD-HTE > HTD-LTE > LTD-HTE > LTD-LTE (b) and HTD-HDT > HTD-LDT > LTD-HDT > LTD-LDT (c) is maintained without much change. This indicates that the task expertise and ten-

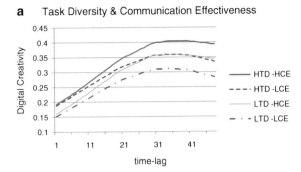

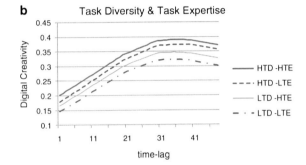

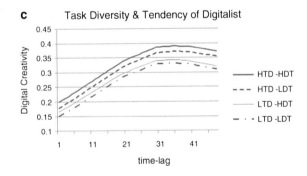

Fig. 3.3 Digital creativity patterns by task diversity. (**a**) Digital creativity patterns by task diversity and communication effectiveness. (**b**) Digital creativity patterns by task diversity and task expertise. (**c**) Digital creativity patterns by task diversity and tendencies of digitalist. *HTD* high task diversity, *LTD* low task diversity, *HCE* high communication effectiveness, *LCE* low communication effectiveness, *HTE* high task expertise, *LTE* low task expertise, *HDT* high digitalist tendency, *LDT* low digitalist tendency

dencies of digitalists are important variables for increasing digital creativity, whether the task diversity is high or low. Moreover, digital creativity is greatly affected by task diversity, so the digital environment needs to be improved in order for the agent to demonstrate high creativity in an environment with high task diversity.

The statistical verification result of each group's longitudinal digital creativity patterns are presented in several tables and figures. Table 3.1 summarizes the simulation results of Fig. 3.3a–c from a time perspective. Table 3.1 also shows the mean value of each group's digital creativity and ranking among four groups on time-lag 1, time-lag 15, time-lag 30, and time-lag 48.

In addition, we analyzed statistical differences in the mean values of each group's digital creativity by conducting ANOVA with SPSS 13.0 in order to assess whether the groups differed in the time-lag perspective. We analyzed statistical differences among the four groups from the perspective of task diversity and communication effectiveness– a group (or teams) with high task diversity (HTD), a group with low task diversity (LTD), a group with high communication effectiveness (HCE), and a group with low communication effectiveness (LCE)—in regards to the mean value of digital creativity on time-lag 1, time-lag 15, time-lag 30, and time-lag 48, respectively. Statistical differences among the four groups in task diversity and task expertise were tested in the same way: a group with task diversity (HTD), a group with low task diversity (LTD), a group with high task expertise (HTE), and a group with low task expertise (LTE). Statistical differences among the four groups in the task diversity and tendency of the digitalist perspective were also tested in the same way: a group with task diversity (HTD), a group with low task diversity (LTD), a group with high digitalist tendency (HDT), and a group with low digitalist tendency (LDT).

The ANOVA results are summarized in Tables 3.2 and 3.3. First, when we consider the test of the homogeneity of variances as seen in Table 3.2, the significance of task diversity and communication effectiveness on four time points—time-lag 1, time-lag 15, time-lag 30, and time-lag 48—are 0.086, 0.167, 0.058, and 0.037, respectively. The significance levels of task diversity and task expertise on the same four time points are 0.131, 0.194, 0.576, and 0.752, respectively. The significance levels of task diversity and tendency of digitalists on the same four time points are 0.445, 0.752, 0.385, and 0.415, respectively. These results indicate that variances in the population are the same, as all significance levels exceed 0.05 with the exception of the case of task diversity and communication effectiveness on time-lag 48.

Secondly, the ANOVA results presented in Table 3.3 show that the significance values of each group on the four time points—time-lag 1, time-lag 15, time-lag 30, and time-lag 48—are lower than 0.05, which indicates that the mean values of digital creativity among HTD, LTD, HCE, and LCE differ, and HTD, LTD, HTE, and LTE also show differences in the mean values of digital creativity. HTD, LTD, HDT, and LDT also show significant differences in the mean values of digital creativity.

Furthermore, Scheffe's posthoc procedure was utilized in order to investigate which combinations of groups have pairwise differences. The results of this test are summarized in Table 3.4.

Table 3.1 Summary of simulations results

Group			Mean of digital creativity				Ranking
			Time-lag = 1	Time-lag = 15	Time-lag = 30	Time-lag = 48	
TD & CE (Fig. 3.3a)	①	HTD HCE	0.1929	0.3019	0.3999	0.3945	Time-lag 1: ①>②>③>④
	②	HTD LCE	0.1889	0.2827	0.3570	0.3357	Time-lag 15: ①>②>③>④
	③	LTD HCE	0.1615	0.2659	0.3566	0.3444	Time-lag 30: ①>②>③>④
	④	LTD LCE	0.1529	0.2414	0.3100	0.2837	Time-lag 48: ①>②>③>④
TD & TE (Fig. 3.3b)	①	HTD HTE	0.2027	0.3019	0.3868	0.3720	Time-lag 1: ①>②>③>④
	②	HTD LTE	0.1800	0.2830	0.3700	0.3576	Time-lag 15: ①>②>③>④
	③	LTD HTE	0.1668	0.2643	0.3452	0.3273	Time-lag 30: ①>②>③>④
	④	LTD LTE	0.1469	0.2426	0.3212	0.3009	Time-lag 48: ①>②>③>④
TD & DT (Fig. 3.3c)	①	HTD HDT	0.1995	0.3002	0.3859	0.3720	Time-lag 1: ①>②>③>④
	②	HTD LDT	0.1790	0.2809	0.3671	0.3541	Time-lag 15: ①>②>③>④
	③	LTD HDT	0.1661	0.2613	0.3401	0.3198	Time-lag 30: ①>②>③>④
	④	LTD LDT	0.1509	0.2485	0.3291	0.3109	Time-lag 48: ①>②>③>④

TD task diversity, *CE* communication effectiveness, *TE* task expertise, *DT* digitalist tendency, *HTD* high task diversity, *LTD* low task diversity, *HCE* high communication effectiveness, *LCE* low communication effectiveness, *HTE* high task expertise, *LTE* low task expertise, *HDT* high digitalist tendency, *LDT* low digitalist tendency

Table 3.2 Test of homogeneity of variances

	Time-lag	Levene statistic	df1	df2	Sig.
TD & CE (Fig. 3.3a)	1	2.227	3	196	0.086
	15	1.708	3	196	0.167
	30	2.538	3	196	0.058
	48	2.876	3	196	0.037
TD & TE (Fig. 3.3b)	1	1.897	3	196	0.131
	15	1.588	3	196	0.194
	30	0.663	3	196	0.576
	48	0.402	3	196	0.752
TD & DT (Fig. 3.3c)	1	0.894	3	196	0.445
	15	0.401	3	196	0.752
	30	1.019	3	196	0.385
	48	0.955	3	196	0.415

TD task diversity, *CE* communication effectiveness, *TE* task expertise, *DT* digitalist tendency

3.5 Concluding Remarks

3.5.1 Discussion

In this study, an individual digitalist was regarded as an agent. The influences of communication effectiveness, task expertise, tendencies of the digitalist with regard to digital creativity, and task diversity (considered as a moderating factor) were analyzed through a MAS approach. The results show that, as time passed, the influences on digital creativity were stronger when communication effectiveness rather than task diversity influenced digital creativity. Task diversity also significantly influenced communication effectiveness, which had a meaningful impact on digital creativity. In addition, task expertise and the tendencies of the digitalist exerted significant influences on digital creativity.

The existing literature indicates that team diversity can have both positive and negative effects on organizational performance. The positive aspects of greater team diversity include generating a wider set of alternatives to decrease group-think, predicting environmental changes more accurately to increase adaptation, and successfully implementing strategic choices through a more procedurally just process [24, 26, 28]. The negative aspects include delayed decision-making, communication breakdowns, and interpersonal conflict [18, 35]. In this study, we found that task diversity positively influences digital creativity. Therefore, organizations should help foster task diversity among their employees in order to increase digital creativity.

This research makes several contributions to theory and practice. In terms of research methodology, the majority of previous research on creativity focused on factors designed to improve creativity and the development of tools to measure creative tendencies through conceptual research. No study utilizing a simulation

Table 3.3 ANOVA table

	Time-lag	Groups	Sum of squares	df	Mean square	F	Sig.
TD & CE	1	Between groups	0.059	3	0.020	58.304	0.000***
		Within groups	0.066	196	$$$$$$$		
		Total	0.124	199			
	15	Between groups	0.097	3	0.032	87.588	0.000***
		Within groups	0.072	196	0.000		
		Total	0.169	199			
	30	Between groups	0.198	3	0.666	152.039	0.000***
		Within groups	0.085	196	0.000		
		Total	0.283	199			
	48	Between groups	0.303	3	0.101	195.710	0.000***
		Within groups	0.101	196	0.001		
		Total	0.404	199			
TD & TE	1	Between groups	0.079	3	0.026	114.478	0.000***
		Within groups	0.045	196	0.000		
		Total	0.124	199			
	15	Between groups	0.094	3	0.031	80.791	0.000***
		Within groups	0.076	196	0.000		
		Total	$$$$$$$	199			
	30	Between groups	0.120	3	0.040	47.646	0.000***
		Within groups	0.164	196	0.001		
		Total	0.283	199			
	48	Between groups	0.147	3	0.049	37.361	0.000***
		Within groups	0.257	196	0.001		
		Total	0.404	199			
TD & DT	1	Between groups	0.072	3	0.024	90.766	0.000***
		Within groups	0.052	196	0.000		
		Total	0.124	199			
	15	Between groups	0.086	3	0.029	67.242	0.000***
		Within groups	0.084	196	0.000		
		Total	0.169	199			
	30	Between groups	0.110	3	0.037	41.260	0.000***
		Within groups	0.174	196	0.001		
		Total	0.283	199			
	48	Between groups	0.134	3	0.045	32.471	0.000***
		Within groups	0.270	196	0.001		
		Total	0.404	199			

TD task diversity, *CE* communication effectiveness, *TE* task expertise, *DT* digitalist tendency
***$p < 0.001$

approach based on a multi-agent system has been conducted to investigate the relationships between elements of the digital environment suitable for the digital age and digital creativity while considering task diversity. For this reason, a new research method using a simulation approach to measure digital creativity considering task diversity was presented in this work. In addition, unlike existing research on

Table 3.4 Result of posthoc test (Scheffe)

	Time-lag	Group1	Group2	Sig.	Difference
TD & CE	1	1(HTD-HCE)	2(HTD-LCE)	0.758	x
			3(LTD-HCE)	0.000**	o
			4(LTD-LCE)	0.000**	o
		2(HTD-LCE)	3(LTD-HCE)	0.000**	o
			4(LTD-LCE)	0.000**	o
		3(LTD-HCE)	4(LTD-LCE)	0.145	x
	15	1(HTD-HCE)	2(HTD-LCE)	0.000**	o
			3(LTD-HCE)	0.000**	o
			4(LTD-LCE)	0.000**	o
		2(HTD-LCE)	3(LTD-HCE)	0.000**	o
			4(LTD-LCE)	0.000**	o
		3(LTD-HCE)	4(LTD-LCE)	0.000**	o
	30	1(HTD-HCE)	2(HTD-LCE)	0.000**	o
			3(LTD-HCE)	0.000**	o
			4(LTD-LCE)	0.000**	o
		2(HTD-LCE)	3(LTD-HCE)	1.000	x
			4(LTD-LCE)	0.000**	o
		3(LTD-HCE)	4(LTD-LCE)	0.000**	o
	48	1(HTD-HCE)	2(HTD-LCE)	0.000**	o
			3(LTD-HCE)	0.000**	o
			4(LTD-LCE)	0.000**	o
		2(HTD-LCE)	3(LTD-HCE)	0.296	x
			4(LTD-LCE)	0.000**	o
		3(LTD-HCE)	4(LTD-LCE)	0.000**	o
TD & TE	1	1(HTD-HTE)	2(HTD-LTE)	0.000**	o
			3(LTD-HTE)	0.000**	o
			4(LTD-LTE)	0.000**	o
		2(HTD-LTE)	3(LTD-HTE)	0.000**	o
			4(LTD-LTE)	0.000**	o
		3(LTD-HTE)	4(LTD-LTE)	0.000**	o
	15	1(HTD-HTE)	2(HTD-LTE)	0.000**	o
			3(LTD-HTE)	0.000**	o
			4(LTD-LTE)	0.000**	o
		2(HTD-LTE)	3(LTD-HTE)	0.000**	o
			4(LTD-LTE)	0.000**	o
		3(LTD-HTE)	4(LTD-LTE)	0.000**	o
	30	1(HTD-HTE)	2(HTD-LTE)	0.041*	o
			3(LTD-HTE)	0.000**	o
			4(LTD-LTE)	0.000**	o
		2(HTD-LTE)	3(LTD-HTE)	0.000**	o
			4(LTD-LTE)	0.000**	o
		3(LTD-HTE)	4(LTD-LTE)	0.001**	o
	48	1(HTD-HTE)	2(HTD-LTE)	0.266	x
			3(LTD-HTE)	0.000**	o
			4(LTD-LTE)	0.000**	o
		2(HTD-LTE)	3(LTD-HTE)	0.001**	o
			4(LTD-LTE)	0.000**	o
		3(LTD-HTE)	4(LTD-LTE)	0.005**	o

(continued)

Table 3.4 (continued)

	Time-lag	Group1	Group2	Sig.	Difference
TD & DT	1	1(HTD-HDT)	2(HTD-LDT)	0.000**	o
			3(LTD-HDT)	0.000**	o
			4(LTD-LDT)	0.000**	o
		2(HTD-LDT)	3(LTD-HDT)	0.005**	o
			4(LTD-LDT)	0.000**	o
		3(LTD-HDT)	4(LTD-LDT)	0.000**	o
	15	1(HTD-HDT)	2(HTD-LDT)	0.000**	o
			3(LTD-HDT)	0.000**	o
			4(LTD-LDT)	0.000**	o
		2(HTD-LDT)	3(LTD-HDT)	0.000**	o
			4(LTD-LDT)	0.000**	o
		3(LTD-HDT)	4(LTD-LDT)	0.027*	o
	30	1(HTD-HDT)	2(HTD-LDT)	0.023*	o
			3(LTD-HDT)	0.000**	o
			4(LTD-LDT)	0.000**	o
		2(HTD-LDT)	3(LTD-HDT)	0.001**	o
			4(LTD-LDT)	0.000**	o
		3(LTD-HDT)	4(LTD-LDT)	0.341	x
	48	1(HTD-HDT)	2(HTD-LDT)	0.133	x
			3(LTD-HDT)	0.000**	o
			4(LTD-LDT)	0.000**	o
		2(HTD-LDT)	3(LTD-HDT)	0.001**	o
			4(LTD-LDT)	0.000**	o
		3(LTD-HDT)	4(LTD-LDT)	0.704	x

TD task diversity, CE communication effectiveness, TE task expertise, DT digitalist tendency, HTD high task diversity, LTD low task diversity, HCE high communication effectiveness, LCE low communication effectiveness, HTE high task expertise, LTE low task expertise, HDT high digitalist tendency, LDT low digitalist tendency
$*p < 0.05$, $**p < 0.01$

creativity, the work outlined here divided task diversity into high and low levels for the evolution pattern analysis of digital creativity over time.

According to the literature, creativity has always promoted organizational performance, a result of a business process that facilitates creativity [41]. Therefore, it is assumed that the more digital creativity improves, the more organizational performance will increase in the digital society. Modern society functions in the context of a knowledge-based economy, indicating that an organization can control its own organizational creativity to produce dramatic organizational change. Lee and Choi [30] are supportive of this premise, showing that the knowledge creation process composed of socialization, externalization, combination, and internalization affects organizational creativity as a whole and positively influences organizational performance.

Based on the results of this study, the following implications for the improvement of future digital creativity and creative thinking were derived. First, it is necessary to create a digital environment that provides members with individual diversity, taking into account task diversity. Second, digital creativity can be improved if knowledge management considering communication effectiveness is vitalized in order to create an environment of creation, accumulation, sharing, utilization, and learning of knowledge. Third, as digital creativity is greatly influenced by the tendencies of the digitalist, it is necessary to improve abilities related to being a digitalist, such as creative thinking, flexibility, change, de-normalization, absorption, and enthusiasm.

3.5.2 Limitations and Further Studies

In this study, elements of digital creativity and their relationships with digital creativity were researched in a simulation using a multi-agent system. Such an approach has its limitations. First, 200 simulations are inadequate to draw adequate conclusions at an organizational level when measuring individual agents. Second, the approach could not be used to suggest an adequate direction considering the size of the organization because the simulation was not performed to reorganize the 300 members of 20 teams in a variety of ways.

Based on the above results, the following directions for future research are proposed. First, this study was more realistic than other research using simulation methods because the simulations were based on the results of verified formulas. However, additional empirical and longitudinal studies considering the passage of time are needed. Second, while this study divided the antecedents of digital creativity into task diversity, communication effectiveness, task expertise, and the tendencies of the digitalist, these elements need to be expanded to various fields.

Acknowledgments This work was supported by the Korea Research Foundation Grant funded by the Korean Government (KRF-2009-342-B00015). This research was also partially supported by WCU (World Class University) program through the National Research Foundation of Korea funded by the Ministry of Education, Science, and Technology (Grant No. R31-2008-000-10062-0).

References

1. Amabile, T.M.: A model of creativity and innovation in organizations. In: Staw, B.M., Cummings, L.L. (eds.) Research in Organizational Behavior, vol. 10, pp. 123–167. JAI Press, Greenwich, CT (1988)
2. Amabile, T.M.: How to kill creativity. Keep doing what you're doing. Or, if you want to spark innovation, rethink how you motivate, reward, and assign work to people. Harv. Bus. Rev. **76**(5), 77–87 (1998)
3. Ashworth, M., Carley, K.: Who you know vs. What You know: The impact of social position and knowledge on team performance. J. Math. Sociol. **30**, 43–75 (2006)
4. Bakker, H., Boersma, K., Oreel, S.: Creativity (Ideas) Management in Industrial R&D Organizations: A crea-political process Model and an empirical illustration of corus RD&T. J. Creat. Innov. Manage. **15**(3), 296–309 (2006)
5. Barrick, M.R., Mount, M.K.: The big five personality dimensions and job performance: A meta-analysis. Pers. Psychol **44**(1), 1–26 (1991)

6. Barrick, M.R., Stewart, G.L., Neubert, M.J., Mount, M.K.: Relating member ability and personality to work-team processes and team effectiveness. J. Appl. Psychol. **83**, 377–391 (1998)
7. Brass, D.: Being in the right place: A structural analysis of individual influence in an organization. Adm. Sci. Q. **26**, 331–348 (1984)
8. Canessa, E., Riolo, R.: An agent-based model of the impact of computer-mediated communication on organizational culture and performance: An example of the application of complex systems analysis tools to the study of CIS. J. Inf. Technol. **21**, 272–283 (2006)
9. Chen, M.H.: Understanding the benefits and detriments of conflict on team creativity process. Creativ. Innov. Manage. **15**(1), 105–116 (2006)
10. Drucker, P.: Post-Capitalist Society. Harper Business, New York (1993)
11. Dubin, R.: Power, function and organization. Pac. Sociol. Rev. **6**, 16–24 (1963)
12. Feldhusen, J.F., Goh, B.E.: Assessing and accessing creativity: An integrative review of theory, research, and development. Creativ. Res. J. **8**(3), 231–247 (1995)
13. Feldhusen, J.F.: Creativity: A knowledge base, meta cognitive skills and personalities factors. J. Creativ. Behav. **29**(4), 255–268 (1995)
14. Giaccardi, E., Fischer, G.: Creativity and evolution: A meta design perspective. Digit. Creativ. **19**(1), 19–32 (2008)
15. Gilbert, N., Troitzsch, K.G.: Simulation for the Social Scientist, 2nd edn. Open University Press, Milton Keynes (2005)
16. Gino, F., Argote, L., Miron-Spektor, E., Todorova, G.: First, get your feet wet: The effects of learning from direct and indirect experience on team creativity. Organ. Behav. Hum. Decis. Process. **111**(2), 102–115 (2010)
17. Hahn, Christian, Fley, Bettina, Florian, Michael, Spresny, Daniela and Fischer, Klaus (2007). 'Social Reputation: a Mechanism for Flexible Self-Regulation of Multiagent Systems'. Journal of Artificial Societies and Social Simulation **10**(1)2. http://jasss.soc.surrey.ac.uk/10/1/2.html
18. Hambrick, D.C., D'Aveni, R.A.: Top team deterioration as part of the downward spiral of large corporate bankruptcies. Manage. Sci. **38**(10), 1445–1466 (1992)
19. Harrison, D.A., Humphrey, S.E.: Designing for diversity or diversity for design? Tasks, interdependence, and within-unit differences at work. J. Organ. Behav. **31**, 328–337 (2010)
20. Harrison, D.A., Price, K.H., Bell, M.P.: Beyond relational demography: Time and the effects of surface-and deep-level diversity on work group cohesion. Acad. Manage. J. **41**(1), 96–107 (1998)
21. Harrison, D.A., Price, K.H., Gavin, J.H., Florey, A.T.: Time, teams, and task performance: Changing effects of surface-and deep-level diversity on group functioning. Acad. Manage. J. **45**(5), 1029–1045 (2002)
22. Hinings, C., Hickson, D., Pennings, J., Schneck, R.: Structural conditions of intraorganizational power. Adm. Sci. Q. **19**, 22–44 (1974)
23. Hogg, L.M.I., Jennings, N.R.: Socially intelligent reasoning for autonomous agents. IEEE Trans. Syst. Man Cybern. Syst. Hum. **31**(5), 381–393 (2001)
24. Jackson, S.E.: Consequences of group composition for the interpersonal dynamics of strategic issue processing. In: Shrivastava, P., Huff, A., Dutton, J. (eds.) Advances in Strategic Management, vol. 8, pp. 345–382. JAI Press, Greenwich, CT (1992)
25. Jehn, K.A., Northcraft, G.B., Neale, M.A.: Why differences make a difference: A field study of diversity, conflict, and performance in workgroups. Adm. Sci. Q. **44**(4), 741–763 (1999)
26. Kim, W., Mauborgne, R.: Implementing global strategies: The role of procedural justice. Strateg. Manage. J. **12**, 125–143 (1991)
27. Kratzer, J., Gemünden, H.G., Lettl, C.: Balancing creativity and time efficiency in multi-team R&D projects: The alignment of formal and informal networks. R&D Manage. **38**(5), 538–549 (2008)
28. Lant, T.K., Milliken, F.J., Batra, B.: The role of managerial learning and interpretation in strategic persistence and reorientation: An empirical exploration. Strateg. Manage. J. **13**(8), 585–608 (1992)
29. Lazaric, N., Raybaut, A.: Knowledge creation facing hierarchy: The dynamics of groups inside the firm. J. Artif. Soc. Soc. Simulat. **7**(2) (2004). http://jasss.soc.surrey.ac.uk/7/2/3.html

30. Lee, H., Choi, B.: Knowledge management enablers, processes, and organizational performance: An integrative view and empirical examination. J. Manage Inf. Syst. **20**(1), 179–228 (2003)
31. Leonard, D., Swap, W.: When Sparks Fly: Igniting Creativity in Group. Harvard Business School Press, Boston (1999)
32. Lubart, T.I.: Creativity. In: Sternberg, R.J. (ed.) Thinking and Problem Solving, pp. 289–332. Academic, London (1994)
33. Mansfield, R.S., Busse, T.V.: The Psychology of Creativity and Discovery: Scientists and Their Work. Nelson-Hall, Chicago (1981)
34. Mellow, E.: The two-conditions view of creativity. J. Creativ. Behav. **30**(2), 126–143 (1996)
35. O'Reilly, C., Snyder, R., Boothe, J.: Effects of executive team demography on organizational change. In: Humber, G., Glick, W. (eds.) Organizational Change and Redesign: Ideas and Insights for Improving Performance, pp. 147–175. Oxford, New York (1993)
36. O'Reilly, C.A., Caldwell, D.F., Barnett, W.P.: Work group demography, social integration, and turnover. Adm. Sci. Q. **34**(1), 21–37 (1989)
37. Palmer, Victor (2006). 'Simulation of the Categorization-Elaboration Model of Diversity and Work-Group Performance'. Journal of Artificial Societies and Social Simulation **9**(3)3. http://jasss.soc.surrey.ac.uk/9/3/3.html
38. Persson, P., Laaksolahti, J., Lonngvist, P.: Understanding socially intelligent agents—A multi-layered phenomenon. IEEE Trans. Syst. Man Cybern. Syst. Hum. **31**(5), 349–360 (2001)
39. Ricchiuto, J.: Collaborative Creativity: Unleashing the Power of Shared Thinking. Oakhill Press, New York (1997)
40. Saunders, R., Gero, J.S.: Artificial creativity: A synthetic approach to the study of creative behaviour. In: Gero, J.S., Maher, M.L. (eds.) Computational and Cognitive Models of Creative Design V, Key Centre of Design Computing and Cognition, pp. 113–139. University of Sydney, Sydney (2001)
41. Sawhney, M., Prandelli, E.: Communities of creation: Managing distributed innovation in turbulent markets. Calif. Manage. Rev. **42**(4), 24–54 (2000)
42. Schelling, T.C.: Micromotives and Macrobehavior. W.W. Norton & Company, Inc. New York, USA (1978)
43. Sole, R., Goodwin, B.: Signs of Life: How Complexity Pervades Biology. Basic Books, New York (2002)
44. Sternberg, R.J., Lubart, T.I.: Defying the Crowd. Cultivating Creativity in a Culture of Conformity. Free Press, New York (1995)
45. Sternberg, R.J.: The Nature of Creativity: Contemporary Psychological Perspectives, pp. 3–7. Cambridge University Press, Cambridge (1988)
46. Stumpf, H.: Scientific creativity: A short overview. Educ. Psychol. Rev. **7**, 225–241 (1995)
47. Taylor, T.: Creativity in evolution: individuals, interactions, and environments. In: Bentley, P.J., Corne, D.W. (eds.) Creative Evolutionary Systems, pp. 79–108. Morgan Kaufmann, San Francisco (2002)
48. Tesluk, P.E., Farr, J.L., Kelin, S.R.: Effect of system's culture and climate on person's creativity. J. Creativ. Behav. **31**(3), 27–41 (1997)
49. Thurow, L.C.: Building Wealth: The New Rules for Individuals, Companies, and Nations in a Knowledge-Based Economy. Harper Collins, New York, USA (1999)
50. Waldrop, M.: Complexity: The Emerging Science at the Edge of Chaos. Simon & Schuster, New York (1992)
51. Williams, W.M., Yang, L.T.: Organizational creativity. In: Sternberg, R.J. (ed.) Handbook of Creativity, pp. 373–391. Cambridge University Press, Cambridge (1999)
52. Woodman, R.W., Sawyer, J.E., Griffin, R.W.: Toward a theory of organizational creativity. Acad. Manage. Rev. **18**(2), 293–321 (1993)
53. Woodman, R.W., Schoenfeldt, L.F.: Individual Differences in Creativity An Inter-actionist Perspective. Handbook of Creativity, pp. 77–92. Plenum Press, New York and London (1989)

Chapter 4
A Creative Generation Task Under Stress: Comparison of a Stress Group with a Non-stress Group

Dae Sung Lee, Kun Chang Lee, and Nam Yong Jo

4.1 Introduction

Many researchers have examined the relationship between stress and creativity in the psychological, organizational, and educational fields, but the form of the relationship remains unclear: Studies have found positive (e.g., [7]), negative (e.g., [1]), and curvilinear (e.g., [30]) relationships between stress and creativity [13]. In order to more objectively assess the effect of stress on creativity, we implemented a physiological approach to studying stress and an experiment for creativity. We used two stress manipulations (threat of shock and performance feedback) with the stress group in this experiment. As physiological signals, we used galvanic skin response (GSR) and electrocardiogram (ECG) data. A total of 31 undergraduate students participated in the study, and the participants were randomly assigned to one of two stress manipulation groups (stress group, $n = 16$; non-stress group, $n = 15$). The subjects were first instructed to meditate for 7 min to obtain baseline GSR and ECG signal data. After the meditation, creativity tasks were given to the subjects, who were asked to generate creative ideas for three different toys in 10 min, and data on their GSR and ECG signals were acquired. After the physiological experiment, the participants completed a questionnaire survey that included stress and creativity items. To confirm the accuracy of the experimental analyses, we investigated whether our stress manipulations corresponded with self-reported stress (using the perceived stress scale [PSS]). In addition, we investigated whether

D.S. Lee • N.Y. Jo
SKK Business School, Sungkyunkwan University,
Seoul 110-745, Republic of Korea
e-mail: leeds1122@gmail.com; namyong.jo@gmail.com

K.C. Lee (✉)
Department of Interaction Science, SKK Business School,
Sungkyunkwan University, Seoul 110-745, Republic of South Korea
e-mail: kunchanglee@gmail.com

K.C. Lee (ed.), *Digital Creativity: Individuals, Groups, and Organizations,*
Integrated Series in Information Systems 32, DOI 10.1007/978-1-4614-5749-7_4,
© Springer Science+Business Media New York 2013

the creativity assessed by experts coincides with self-reported creativity. If there were disagreements between the methods, we explored the implications of the results. We first review existing studies on stress and creativity, and then explain the experiments and present the research results along with our interpretations.

4.2 Theoretical Background

4.2.1 Creativity and Creative Generation Task

Creativity is a complex concept that has been discussed by researchers in a variety of ways [40], but has generally been defined as a judgment of the novelty and usefulness (or value) of something [24]. In other words, creativity can be defined as any process used to generate creative outcomes based on the ability to produce something new [2]. In this respect, creative thinking generates new ideas and novel solutions to problems, and is critical for adapting to changing surroundings. Many special endeavors, such as developing inventions, writing, or research and development (R&D) require creative thinking [42]. In our study, subjects were asked to produce three novel ideas within a limited time. This idea-generation task required creative thinking because it involved generating novel ideas using subjects' imaginations.

4.2.2 The Relationship Between Stress and Creativity

In many studies, the effect of stress on performance has been explained by an inverted U-shaped (curvilinear) relationship. In other words, some degree of stress may help an individual maintain concentration on a task with excitement. Reviewing the literature on the relationship between stress and creativity, we found negative, positive, and curvilinear relationships.

4.2.2.1 Negative Effect

In view of distraction arousal theory [43], stress is negatively related to creativity performance. Due to limited mental resources, people use some of these resources to deal with stress. Therefore, they use fewer cognitive resources for other tasks [13]. The decrease in cognitive resources may also lead to simpler cognitive strategies, such as using a narrow attentional focus [23]. Simple cognitive strategies may produce more common and less original ideas [9, 20]. In sum, stress has a negative effect on creativity by demanding fewer cognitive resources that are not available for creative thinking. Accordingly, people employ simpler cognitive strategies that may undermine creativity [13].

4.2.2.2 Positive Effect

Some theories propose that stress is positively related to creativity. Stress brings about creative thought and motivates people to find solutions to problems (e.g., [4, 34]). If individuals are exposed to stress, they may use problem-solving strategies, which can lead to enhanced creativity [12]. Stress can have a positive effect on creativity by demanding creative solutions and providing cognitive stimulation and motivational arousal for creative thinking [5, 36].

4.2.2.3 Curvilinear Effect

Some researchers have suggested another alternative for the relationship between stressors and creativity [6], where stress is curvilinearly related to creativity (e.g., [45]). Activation theory (e.g., [25]) posits that stress can enhance performance up to a certain threshold, but that too much activation restricts performance, particularly for complex tasks such as creative tasks. At a moderate level of activation, individuals may be the most creative. The moderate activation level increases task engagement and leads to the optimal use of cognitive resources by lowering negative affect (e.g., [8, 25]). Conversely, too little or too much activation may bring about a lack of engagement and cognitive interference, possibly disturbing performance for cognitively demanding tasks. Given that cognitive, emotional, and behavioral engagement are important processes for creativity [19], a moderate level of activation leads to the most creativity [13].

In the present study we define stress as distress, or stress that has reached a level at which it is negatively related to a creative task. Our experiment employs two stress manipulations (threat of shock and performance feedback) in a specific group. Studies using a stimulus approach are concerned with stressors; that is, physical or psychological conditions that necessitate an adaptive response [27, 31]. Creativity is the production of ideas, solutions, or products that are novel and useful in a given situation [3]. A product-based approach to creativity is the most generally accepted. Thus, our participants are asked to implement creativity tasks through creative thinking in order to investigate the relationship between stress and creativity.

4.2.3 Stress Tests

4.2.3.1 Self-Reported Assessment

The stress response is measured and evaluated in terms of perceptual, behavioral, and physical responses. The assessment of perceptual responses to a stressor entails subjective estimations and perceptions, and self-reported questionnaires are the most popular instruments used to measure stress [16]. Representative measures are the PSS [15], the Life Events and Coping Inventory (LECI) [18], and the Stress Response Inventory (SRI) [28]. In our study, we selected the PSS.

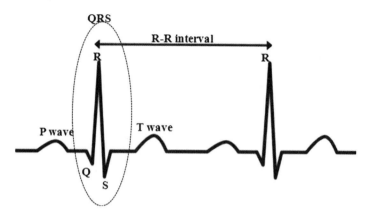

Fig. 4.1 ECG results of the structural model

4.2.3.2 Physiological Assessment

The physical response to stress has two components: a physiological response indicative of central-autonomic activity and a biochemical response involving changes in the endocrine and immune systems [16]. Stress induces a change in autonomic functioning [44], influencing blood pressure and heart rate and reflecting a predominance of sympathetic nervous system activity [37]. An ECG (Electrocardiogram) is a recorded tracing of the electrical activity generated by the heart. Figure 4.1 shows a P wave, a QRS complex, and a T wave in the ECG. The P wave represents a trial depolarization, the QRS represents ventricular depolarization, and the T wave reflects the rapid repolarization of the ventricles [21]. The R-R interval is the time interval between two R peaks and is used to calculate heart rate.

Heart rate variability (HRV) is beat-to-beat variation in the heart rate, and has recently been used as a biomarker of autonomic nervous system (ANS) activity associated with mental stress [46]. HRV analysis is generally divided into two methods: time-domain and frequency-domain. The time-domain analysis of HRV represents quantifying the mean or standard deviation of R-R intervals. Frequency-domain analysis involves calculating the power of the respiratory-dependent high frequency (HF) and low frequency (LF) components of HRV. In this study, we selected the standard deviation of R-R intervals (SDNN) and LF/HF ratio as ECG information. Mental stress is reported as giving rise to a decrease in the high-frequency component and an increase in the low-frequency component of HRV [10]. Therefore, the LF/HF ratio increases if mental stress increases. On the other hand, mental stress evokes a decrease in SDNN. GSR is a measure of the electrical resistance of the skin. A transient increase in skin conductance is proportional to sweat secretion [17]. When an individual is under mental stress, sweat-gland activity is activated, increasing skin conductance. The sweat glands are also controlled by the SNS (Sympathetic Nervous System), so skin conductance acts as an indicator for sympathetic activation due to stress reactions.

4.3   Method

4.3.1   Subjects

We recruited 37 healthy participants among undergraduate students at a South Korean university. Prior to the experiment, the subjects were given written and verbal information explaining the experimental procedures. Through interviews, we confirmed that none of the students used medication for hypertension or any other cardiovascular disease and that they were all free of any nervous or other psychological disorder. We received written informed consent from all subjects and each student was paid 20,000 Korean won for participation. Among them, six subjects with corrupted data were eliminated from the experiment. A total of 31 subjects (22 men and 9 women) were thus used in the data analysis. The mean age of the participants was 22 years (range of 18–26 years). Some of the subjects were randomly assigned to the stress manipulation group, while others were in the non-stress manipulation group (stress group, $n = 16$; non-stress group, $n = 15$).

4.3.2   Experiment

Prior to the physiological measurements, subjects were asked to cleanse their hands and remove all accessories from their body. Then, the subjects were instructed to sit comfortably and keep their left hand still as the experiment started. Each subject was instructed to attach two GSR electrodes to the index and middle fingers of the left hand and place three ECG electrodes on the chest and abdomen. We used a Biopac MP100 series for measurement and AcqKnowledge 4.1 for the analysis. After the GSR and ECG signals showed normal waves, the subjects were asked to meditate for 7 min to obtain baseline data on the GSR and ECG signals. The creativity tasks were then delivered to the participants, who were instructed to produce creative ideas for three different toys in 10 min. At the same time, the subjects were shown examples used by Smith et al. [42]. In the course of task implementation, GSR and ECG signals were measured for both the stress and non-stress groups, but the stress manipulations were given only to the stress group. After the physiological experiment, the subjects were asked to complete the questionnaire survey, which consisted of stress and creativity items.

4.3.2.1   Creative Generation Task

In order to generate ideas for new toys, the subjects were instructed to sketch and label three novel ideas within 10 min. They were told, "Imagine that you are employed by a toy company which is in need of new ideas for toys. Within 10 min, draw three different toys of your own creative designs. Duplication of toys that currently exist or have already existed is not permitted." This script was quoted from Smith et al. [42].

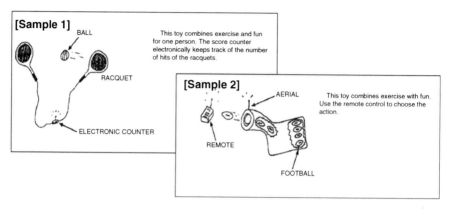

Fig. 4.2 Samples for creative generation task

4.3.2.2 Stress Manipulation

We employed two stress manipulations (threat of shock and performance feedback) with the stress group. The two stress manipulations were used by Bogdan and Pizzagalli [11]. In case of the threat-of-shock manipulation (no shock was ever actually delivered), the subjects were informed of the possibility that they would receive an "unpleasant but not painful" electrical shock through the electrodes attached to their body. In other words, the participants were asked whether the possibility that they would receive a shock was dependent upon their performance in comparison to past subjects. In the performance-feedback manipulation, the subjects were told that they must be lacking in creativity and be less creative than previous participants. These manipulations were implemented according to a fixed pattern, independent of actual performance.

4.3.2.3 Questionnaire Survey

To compare manipulated stress in the experiment with perceived stress, we selected PSS as the survey item [14, 15]. The PSS measures the degree to which situations are considered stressful by addressing events experienced beforehand. It was designed to quantify how unpredictable, uncontrollable, and overloaded adults find their lives. We conducted another survey to see whether self-reported creativity [35, 39] agreed with actual creative performance. Each item in our survey was measured on a 7-point Likert scale, with answers ranging from "strongly disagree" (1) to "strongly agree" (7). The items in the survey were developed by adopting existing measures validated by other researchers. Self-reported creative performance was measured with three items developed by Oldham and Cummings [35]. The items ($\alpha=0.928$) asked subjects to rate the level of creativity and originality in the work they produced. Perceived stress was measured with 10 items ($\alpha=0.863$).

Fig. 4.3 Experiment for ECG and GRS

4.3.3 Statistical Analysis

To assess the physiological signals and creativity, the differences between the stress group and non-stress groups were analyzed using the Mann–Whitney U Test. This test was performed to test the null hypothesis that the stress group is not different from the non-stress group. The results from the Mann–Whitney U Test are presented along with the p-values. Statistical significance was assumed for a level of $p < 0.05$. We examined the two types of creativity ratings for each group with the Wilcoxon signed ranks test. Finally, we investigated the relationship between stress and creativity in the descriptive statistics.

4.4 Results

4.4.1 Comparison of the Stress Group with the Non-stress Group

4.4.1.1 Physiological Signals and Creativity Assessment

The relationship between manipulated stress and physiological signals (Normalized ΔGSR, ΔSDNN, and ΔLF/HF ratio) was examined using the Mann–Whitney U Test. This test is one of the most powerful nonparametric tests, and is a useful alternative to the parametric test when the researcher wishes to avoid the t-test's assumptions or when the sample sizes are relatively small [41]. Though there was no significant difference between the stress group and non-stress group in the normalized

Table 4.1 Construct and measurement

Constructs	Items	Measurement	Literatures
Stress	S1	In this experiment, how have you been upset because of something that happened unexpectedly?	Cohen et al. [15]
	S2	In this experiment, how have you felt that you were unable to control the important things?	
	S3	In this experiment, how have you felt nervous and stressed?	
	S4	In this experiment, how have you felt confident about your ability to handle your personal problems? (Reverse)	
	S5	In this experiment, how have you felt that things were going your way? (Reverse)	
	S6	In this experiment, how have you found that you could not cope with all the things that you had to do?	
	S7	In this experiment, how have you been able to control irritations? (Reverse)	
	S8	In this experiment, how have you felt that you were on top of things? (Reverse)	
	S9	In this experiment, how have you been angered because of things that were outside of your control?	
	S10	In this experiment, how have you felt difficulties were piling up so high that you could not overcome them?	
Creative performance	C1	The work I produce is creative	Shalley et al. [39]
	C2	The work I produce is original	
	C3	The work I produce is novel	

ΔGSR and ΔSDNN, as shown in Table 4.2, we confirmed that the stress group had a higher ΔLF/HF ratio value than the non-stress group, with a statistically significant difference. On the other hand, the creativity assessed by experts did not have a statistically significant result.

4.4.1.2 Creativity Assessment by Experts

Subjects' creative tasks were assessed by three experts who had previously published papers on creativity. Assessment criteria were the components (creative, original, and novel) of self-reported creative performance developed by Oldham and Cummings [35]. We tested whether the assessments were appropriate using the within-rater agreement statistic (rwg [26]) and used intraclass correlation coefficients, ICC(1) and ICC(K), to estimate raters' similarity [33]. The mean rwg of 0.933 indicated a high level of agreement among judges on rating the internal team environment; the ICC(1) of 0.820 demonstrated that raters did not show significant variance; and the ICC(K) of 0.932 suggested that the assessments were reliable.

Table 4.2 Mann–Whitney U test results (1)

Group	N	Normalized ΔGSR		Normalized ΔSDNN	
		Mean	SD	Mean	SD
Stress	16	0.006	0.164	0.022	0.313
Non-stress	15	−0.043	0.233	0.237	0.814
Total	31	−0.018	0.199	0.126	0.608
Two-tailed probability		0.54		0.678	

Group	N	Normalized ΔLF/HF ratio		Creativity assessed by experts	
		Mean	SD	Mean	SD
Stress	16	1.176	1.706	3.41	0.734
Non-stress	15	0.262	0.845	3.081	0.862
Total	31	0.734	1.416	3.251	0.803
Two-tailed probability		**0.036***		0.373	

*Statistically significant at $p < 0.05$

4.4.1.3 Self-Reported Stress and Creative Performance

Statistically significant differences between the two groups were observed for perceived stress, but not for self-reported creative performance. This result shows that our manipulation of stress was well controlled in the experiment and discriminates the stress group from the other group.

4.4.2 Relationship Between Stress and Creativity

4.4.2.1 The Two Types of Creativity Ratings for Each Group

Though we did not confirm the difference between the two groups for creativity through the Mann–Whitney U Test, we verified that the stress group experienced more perceived stress than the other, as shown in Table 4.3. Accordingly, the subjects appear to have been properly divided. Therefore, we confirmed which group could separately explain creativity by comparing the creativity assessed by experts and self-reported creativity. Table 4.4 shows that there was a discrepancy between the assessments of experts and the self-reported ratings within the stress group on creative performance, according to the Wilcoxon signed ranks test. In the non-stress group, the two ratings for creative performance were not significantly different. Judging from this result, self-reported creativity in the stress group might be influenced by the manipulated stress. In the next section, these points are further discussed.

Table 4.3 Mann–Whitney U test results (2)

Group	N	Perceived stress		Self-reported creative performance	
		Mean	SD	Mean	SD
Stress	16	4.388	1.23	2.708	1.134
Non-stress	15	3.34	0.912	3.244	1.63
Total	31	3.881	1.195	2.968	1.399
Two-tailed probability		**0.016***		0.349	

*Statistically significant at $p < 0.05$

Table 4.4 Wilcoxon signed ranks test of creativity for each group

Stress group

		N	Mean rank	Sum of ranks
Negative ranks	(SC < EC)	12	9.208	110.5
Positive ranks	(SC > EC)	4	6.375	25.5
Ties	(SC = EC)	0		
Total		16		
$Z = -2.198$		Two-tailed probability = 0.028*		

Non-stress group

		N	Mean rank	Sum of ranks
Negative ranks	(SC < EC)	8	6.625	53
Positive ranks	(SC > EC)	7	9.571	67
Ties	(SC = EC)	0		
Total		15		
$Z = -0.398$		Two-tailed probability = 0.691		

SC self-reported creative performance, EC creativity assessed by experts
*Statistically significant at $p < 0.05$

4.4.2.2 Descriptive Statistics for the Two Types of Creativity Ratings

As shown in Table 4.5 and Fig. 4.4, self-reported creativity in the stress group (mean = 2.708; median = 2.833) was relatively lower than that in the non-stress group (mean = 3.244; median = 3.333), while creativity in the stress group as assessed by experts (mean = 3.410; median = 3.333) was relatively higher than that assessed by experts for the non-stress group (mean = 3.081; median = 3.222) (Table 4.6).

4.5 Discussion

When we reviewed the mean values of the results, the stress group had a higher normalized ΔGSR, a lower normalized ΔSDNN, and a higher normalized ΔLF/HF ratio than the non-stress group. However, only the normalized ΔLF/HF ratio had statistical significance. The descriptive statistics of the physiological signals

Table 4.5 Descriptive statistics for creativity

	Group	Mean	Median	SD	Max	Min
Creativity assessed by experts	Stress	3.41	3.333	0.734	4.556	2.222
	Non	3.081	3.222	0.862	4.556	1.444
Self-reported creative performance	Stress	2.708	2.833	1.134	4.333	1
	Non	3.244	3.333	1.63	6	1

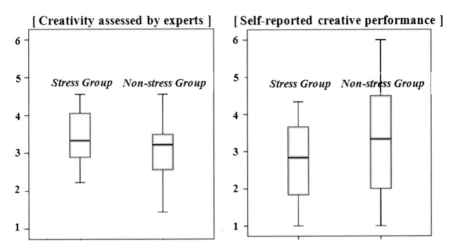

Fig. 4.4 Box plot for creativity

indicated that the stress group experienced mental stress during the experiment. Many published papers have selected the ΔLF/HF ratio as an important biomarker of ANS activity associated with mental stress [46]. GSR might not be a critical indicator of mental stress because sweat-gland activity could be related to ethnic origin [29]. Therefore, the subjects are thought to be properly divided. While some researchers have explained the curvilinear relationship of stress and performance, the negative effects of stress become magnified under conditions of acute stress, or stress with sudden, novel, intense, and relatively short duration [38]. With the threat of shock and negative performance feedback in our experiment, acute stress negatively affects mental models and transactional memory, explaining poorer performance through information-processing theory [22]. Distraction arousal theory [43] proposes that stress has a negative effect on creativity performance. Due to limited mental resources, people use fewer cognitive resources for other tasks [13]. The stress group had a lower level of self-reported creative performance than the non-stress group in the experiment, aside from statistical significance. However, the negative relationship between stress and creativity may be questionable, because the stress group's self-reported creativity could be influenced by the negative performance feedback introduced in the experiment. On the other hand, judging from experts' assessments, the stress group showed relatively strong creativity. Namely,

Table 4.6 Stem-and-leaf plot for creativity

Creativity assessed by experts

Stress group		Non-stress group	
Frequency	Stem and leaf	Frequency	Stem and leaf
2	2 . 24	2	1.48
3	2.688	4	2.2557
3	3.001	7	3.223368
3	3.566	2	4.35
4	4.0134		
1	4.5		
16		15	

Self-reported creative performance

Stress group		Non-stress group	
Frequency	Stem and leaf	Frequency	Stem and leaf
3	1.003	2	1.00
1	1.6	5	2.00000
4	2.0003	1	3.3
1	2.6	4	4.0036
3	3.003	2	5.03
1	3.6	1	6.0
3	4.033		
16		15	

Stem width: 1, each leaf: 1 case

the non-stress group was evaluated as being at a level lower than the stress group in the experiment, aside from statistical significance. Some studies suggest that stress evokes creative thought and motivates people to find solutions to problems (e.g., [4, 34]). Stress encourages individuals to use problem-solving strategies, leading to enhanced creativity [12]. On the other hand, Nicol and Long [34] found no relationship between creative thinking and stress among music therapists. In view of various studies (showing negative, positive, curvilinear, and indifferent relationships between stress and creativity), the effect of stressors on creativity are more complex than previously assumed and point to the need to better understand the boundary conditions that shed light on inconsistent findings [32, 34]. Therefore, we should consider the effects of more detailed factors and surroundings on stress and creativity in future studies. In future research, we could investigate other stressors, rather than negative performance feedback, and how these may affect self-reported measures. We did not find the relationship between stress and creativity to have statistical significance. Thus, we should obtain larger samples for experimentation and consider other factors that might impact stress and creativity in order to induce various and delicate interpretations.

Acknowledgments This work was supported by the Korea Research Foundation Grant funded by the Korean Government (KRF-2009-342-B00015).

References

1. Amabile, T.M., Goldfarb, P., Brackfield, S.C.: Social influences on creativity: Evaluation, coaction, and surveillance. Creativity Res. J. **3**(1), 6–21 (1990)
2. Amabile, T.M.: A model of creativity and innovation in organizations. Res. Organ. Behav. **10**, 123–167 (1988)
3. Amabile, T.M.: Creativity in Context: Update to the Social Psychology of Creativity. Westview Press, Boulder, CO (1996)
4. Anderson, N., De Dreu, C.K.W., Nijstad, B.A.: The Routinization of innovation research: A constructively critical review of the state-of-the-science. J. Organ. Behav. **25**(2), 147–173 (2004)
5. Andrews, F.M., Farris, G.F.: Time pressure and performance of scientists and engineers: A five-year panel study. Organ. Behav. Hum. Decis. Process. **8**(2), 185–200 (1972)
6. Avey, J.B., Luthans, F., Hannah, S.T., Sweetman, D., Peterson, C.: Impact of employees' character strengths of wisdom on stress and creative performance. Hum. Res. Manage. J. (2011). doi:10.1111/j.1748-8583.2010.00157.x
7. Baer, J.R.: Gender differences in the effects of extrinsic motivation on creativity. J. Creative Behav. **32**(1), 18–37 (1998)
8. Baer, M., Oldham, G.R.: The curvilinear relation between experienced creative time pressure and creativity: Moderating effects of openness to experience and support for creativity. J. Appl. Psychol. **91**(4), 963–970 (2006)
9. Baron, R.S.: Distraction-conflict theory: Progress and problems. Adv. Exp. Soc. Psychol. **19**, 1–39 (1986)
10. Bernardi, L., Wdowczyk-Szulc, J., Valenti, C., Castoldi, S., Passino, C., Spadacini, G., Sleight, P.: Effects of controlled breathing, mental activity, and mental stress with or without verbalization on heart rate variability. J. Am. Coll. Cardiol. **35**(6), 1462–1469 (2000)
11. Bogdan, R., Pizzagalli, D.A.: Acute stress reduces reward responsiveness: Implications for depression. Biol. Psychiatry **60**(10), 1147–1154 (2006)
12. Bunce, D., West, M.: Changing work environments, innovative coping responses to occupational stress. Work Stress **8**(4), 319–331 (1994)
13. Byron, K., Khazanchi, S., Nazarian, D.: The relationship between stressors and creativity: A meta-analysis examining competing theoretical models. J. Appl. Psychol. **95**(1), 201–212 (2010)
14. Cohen, S., Williamson, G.: Perceived stress in a probability sample of the United States. In: Spacapan, S., Oskamp, S. (eds.) The Social Psychology of Health. Sage, Newbury Park, CA (1988)
15. Cohen, S., Kamarck, T., Mermelstein, R.: A global measure of perceived stress. J. Health Soc. Behav. **24**, 386–396 (1983)
16. Cohen, S., Kessler, R., Gordon, L.: Measuring Stress—A Guide for Health and Social Scientists. Oxford University Press, New York (1997)
17. Darrow, C.: The rationale for treating the change in galvanic skin response as a change in conductance. Psychophysiology **1**(1), 31–38 (1964)
18. Dise-Lewis, J.E.: The life events and coping inventory: An assessment of stress in children. Psychosom. Med. **50**, 484–499 (1988)
19. Drazin, R., Glynn, M.A., Kazanjian, R.K.: Multilevel theorizing about creativity in organizations: A sensemaking perspective. Acad. Manage. Rev. **24**(2), 286–307 (1999)
20. Drwal, R.L.: The influence of psychological stress upon creative thinking. Pol. Psychol. Bull. **4**, 125–129 (1973)
21. Dubin, D.: Rapid Interpretation of EKG's. Cover Publishing, Tampa, Florida (2000)
22. Ellis, A.P.J.: System breakdown: The role of mental models and transactive memory in the relationship between acute stress and team performance. Acad. Manage. J. **49**(3), 576–589 (2006)
23. Eysenck, H.J.: Genius: The Natural History of Creativity. Cambridge University Press, Cambridge, MA (1995)

24. Ford, C.M.: A theory of individual creative action in multiple social domains. Acad. Manage. Rev. **21**(4), 1112–1142 (1996)
25. Gardner, D.G.: Activation theory and task design: An empirical test of several new predictions. J. Appl. Psychol. **71**(3), 411–418 (1986)
26. James, L.R., Demaree, R.G., Wolf, G.: rWG: An assessment of within-group interrater agreement. J. Appl. Psychol. **78**, 306–309 (1993)
27. Jex, S.M., Beehr, T.A., Roberts, C.K.: The meaning of occupational stress items to survey respondents. J. Appl. Psychol. **77**(5), 623–628 (1992)
28. Koh, K., Park, J., Kim, C., Cho, S.: Development of the stress response inventory and its application in clinical practice. Psychosom. Med. **63**, 668–678 (2001)
29. Kugelmass, S., Lieblich, I.: Effects of realistic stress and procedural interference in experimental lie detection. J. Appl. Psychol. **50**(3), 211–216 (1966)
30. Landon, P.B., Suedfeld, P.: Complex cognitive performance and sensory deprivation: Completing the U-curve. Percept. Mot. Skills **34**(2), 601–602 (1972)
31. LePine, J.A., Podsakoff, N.P., LePine, M.A.: A meta-analytic test of the challenge stressor-hindrance stressor framework: An explanation for inconsistent relationships among stressors and performance. Acad. Manage. J. **48**, 764–775 (2005)
32. Marsh, R.L., Landau, J.D., Hicks, J.L.: How examples may (and may not) constrain creativity. Mem. Cognit. **24**(5), 669–680 (1996)
33. McGraw, K.O., Wong, S.P.: Forming inferences about some intraclass correlation coefficients. Psychol. Methods **1**, 30–46 (1996)
34. Nicol, J.J., Long, B.C.: Creativity and perceived stress of female music therapists and hobbyists. Creativity Res. J. **9**(1), 1–10 (1996)
35. Oldham, G.R., Cummings, A.: Employee creativity: Personal and contextual factors at work. Acad. Manage. J. **39**, 607–634 (1996)
36. Pelz, D.C.: Creative tensions in the research and development climate. In: Katz, R. (ed.) Managing Professionals in Innovative Organizations: A Collection of Readings, pp. 37–48. Ballinger, New York (1988)
37. Ritvanen, T., Louhevaara, V., Helin, P., Vaisanen, S., Hanninen, O.: Responses of the autonomic nervous system during periods of perceived high and low work stress in younger and older female teachers. Appl. Ergon. **37**, 311–318 (2005)
38. Salas, E., Driskell, J.E., Hughes, S.: Introduction: The study of stress and human performance. In: Driskell, J.E., Salas, E. (eds.) Stress and Human Performance. Erlbaum, Mahwah, NJ (1996)
39. Shalley, C.E., Gilson, L.L., Blum, T.C.: Interactive effects of growth need strength, self-reported creative performance. Acad. Manage. J. **52**(3), 489–505 (2009)
40. Shalley, C.E., Gilson, L., Blum, T.C.: Matching creativity requirements and the work environment: Effects on satisfaction and intentions to leave. Acad. Manage. J. **43**(2), 215–223 (2000)
41. Siegel, S., Castellan, N.J.: Nonparametric Statistics for the Behavioural Sciences. McGraw-Hill, New York (1988)
42. Smith, S.M., Ward, T.B., Schumacher, J.S.: Constraining effects of examples in a creative generation task. Mem. Cognit. **21**(6), 837–845 (1993)
43. Teichner, W.H., Arees, E., Reilly, R.: Noise and human performance: A psychophysiological approach. Ergonomics **6**(1), 83–97 (1963)
44. Van der Kar, L.D., Blair, M.L.: Forebrain pathways mediating stress induced hormone secretion. Front. Neuroendocrinol. **20**, 41–48 (1999)
45. Yerkes, R.M., Dodson, J.D.: The relation of strength of stimulus to rapidity of habit-formation. J. Comp. Neurol. Psychol. **18**(5), 459–482 (1908)
46. Zhong, X., Hilton, H.J., Gates, G.J., Jelic, S., Stern, Y., Bartels, M.N., DeMeersman, R.E., Basner, R.C.: Increased sympathetic and decreased parasympathetic cardiovascular modulation in normal humans with acute sleep deprivation. J. Appl. Physiol. **98**(6), 2024–2032 (2005)

Chapter 5
Exploring the Revelation Process for Individual Creativity Based on Exploitation and Exploration: A Physiological Experiment Approach

Seong Wook Chae, Kun Chang Lee, and Min Hee Hahn

5.1 Introduction

In the rapidly changing, competitive business environment, creativity is more important than ever as a necessary survival factor for organizational competitive advantage, and studies on creativity have recently drawn attention [1, 2]. It is possible to improve the quality of decision-making by exercising creativity [3], and a decision support system (DSS) makes it possible to effectively exercise creativity in order to make better decisions [4].

The process of attaining a creative outcome involves implementing creative activities through exploration and exploitation. Exploitation is characterized by occurrences in a relatively short period of time, with high certainty and guaranteed stabilized achievements, whereas exploration is characterized by difficult occurrences within a short period of time and high uncertainty. Exploitation can be effective in the short term, but if attention is not paid to exploration, competitiveness weakens in the long term [5]. Exploration is not recommended at all times and in all situations, and exploitation does not need to be avoided at all times. Which to use, and when, depends on the situation, and a balance needs to be struck between the

S.W. Chae
SKK Business School, Management Research Institute, Sungkyunkwan University,
Seoul 110-745, Republic of Korea
e-mail: seongwookchae@gmail.com

K.C. Lee (✉)
Department of Interaction Science, SKK Business School, Sungkyunkwan University,
Seoul 110-745, Republic of South Korea
e-mail: kunchanglee@gmail.com

M.H. Hahn
SKK Business School, Sungkyunkwan University, Seoul 110-745, Republic of Korea
e-mail: minheehahn@gmail.com

K.C. Lee (ed.), *Digital Creativity: Individuals, Groups, and Organizations*,
Integrated Series in Information Systems 32, DOI 10.1007/978-1-4614-5749-7_5,
© Springer Science+Business Media New York 2013

two. However, exploitation is sometimes more necessary than exploration, and vice versa. If the environment requires a creative outcome, it may be necessary to facilitate explorative activities. In order to effectively induce the individual creativity desired by an organization, it is necessary to take a look at how individuals conduct explorative and exploitative activities in specific circumstances.

Studies on creativity have been conducted through the use of self-reported questionnaire data [6, 7], and most pertain to conscientized responses or measurement based on memories and arguments. For this reason, they can result in cognitive distortion and may not always provide objective information. In addition, as it is only possible to know the potential responses experienced by a subject in the course of resolution to a task, there are limitations in figuring out why such responses were generated. Specifically, in the case of analyzing self-reported data, a respondent's activity in the past (or characteristic behavior), mental state such as conduct, tension, and motivation, and cognitive confirmation of external environment variables require a higher cognitive level to answer as compared with collecting demographic data such as age and gender [8]. It is not easy to ensure the accuracy of these more involved measurements and they are more likely to be biased. To cope with these limitations, we employed physiological signals that occur in the course of exercising creativity on the part of an individual in order to objectively assess psychological and physical changes. Measuring physiological signals is one of the best ways to immediately acquire information on actual changes in the subject during the course of a test without interruptions on the part of the subject.

The present study starts with a question on how to maximize the manifestation of creativity, which is crucial for individual and organizational success in daily decision-making and in the information system environment that has become a part of everyday life. In order to answer this question, the study focuses on complementing weaknesses using self-reported questionnaire data by applying physiological signals, where the subject's response can be objectively and scientifically acquired through galvanic skin responses (GSRs) and electrocardiogram. The purpose of this study is to understand how task difficulty and emotion, as sources of stress, affect creativity manifestation activities such as exploration and exploitation in the DSS environment. Toward this end, the individual task resolution situation was manipulated based on two levels and two factors through a test design, and physiological signals were measured in order to acquire objective results.

5.2   Theoretical Background

5.2.1   Creativity

Creativity is generally defined as the outcome of a new, useful idea and a resolution to a problem. It is also referred to as a process of creating an idea or resolving a problem as well as an actual idea or resolution itself [9, 10]. Regarding the newness and usefulness of creativity, Simonton stated that a variation process stems from the newness of an idea and that a selection process is caused by the usefulness of an idea. The newness that is a key factor of creativity is mostly determined by cognitive changes [11]. The more cognitive changes one has, the more likely that individual is to be creative. Affect is cited as one of the sources of such cognitive changes and is closely related to creativity. According to existing studies on creativity and emotion, a positive sentiment that stimulates creativity elicits cognitive changes that stimulate further creativity [12], and positive emotion then expands the scope of cognition and attention [13]. A positive mood further increases performance related to creativity [14]. Moreover, creativity is known to improve performance on various tasks, including decision-making, which generally includes a series of phases and procedures in which creativity is useful. Creativity can be improved through the DSS.

5.2.2 Exploration and Exploitation

The exploration and exploitation concepts introduced by March are very important mechanisms in organizational growth and survival. Exploration can be explained through the use of terms such as search, variation, risk-taking, experimentation, play, flexibility, discovery, and innovation, and exploitation refers to refinement, choice, production, efficiency, selection, implementation, and execution. Exploration involves pursuing changes, taking risks, and pushing for experiments, and exploitation tends to reduce changes and is aimed at efficiency [5].

The approaches to exploration and exploitation have mainly been taken studies of organizations [5], but the concepts are also discussed in terms of the process of producing creative or innovative outcomes [15, 16]. Audia and Goncalo [15] divided creativity into divergent creativity and incremental creativity, explaining divergent creativity by linking it with exploratory activities while elucidating incremental creativity by connecting it to exploitation activities. Benner and Tushman [16] divided innovation into exploratory and exploitative innovation. Exploratory innovation is exploring new competences and developing other technological trajectories in addition to the existing technological trajectory owned by an organization. Exploitative innovation is referred to as innovation that improves technology based on an existing technological trajectory.

5.2.3 Task Difficulty

Task difficulty is referred to as the difficulty level of an activity requiring significant cognitive or physical efforts to develop knowledge and technology on the part of learners [17]. If the task difficulty is high, an individual faces a task or situation where he or she needs to use higher levels of knowledge and technology than his or her current level of competence. In addition, an individual is not motivated by a task whose success or failure is certain, but is motivated by circumstances where the rate of success in completing a task is predicted at an appropriate level and has a sense of challenge [18]. Determining the task difficulty is not only necessary to design and develop a task, but is also important to understand the result of a task. Task difficulty has been studied intensively in the areas of psychology and pedagogy with regard to socialization and language acquisition since the 1980s. Candlin suggested a series of standards to differentiate the difficulty of tasks, such as cognitive load, task objectives, and code complexity [19]. Skehan presented three types of differentiation to analyze task difficulty by combining Candlin's standard with a cognitive approach model of language learning: code complexity, communication stress, and cognitive complexity [20].

5.2.4 *Physiological Signal*

If a human being is physically stimulated, feeling sick, or feeling hot or exhausted, physical changes tend to occur. The human body is affected by the emotional stimulation of thinking and feeling in addition to physical stimulation. Previous studies have shown that emotional stimulation leads to emotional awakening, and the state of awakening is closely related to the response of the sympathetic system [21, 22]. For example, if a person is exposed to a stress factor, the human body tends to save strength and energy to resist or adapt while facilitating the sympathetic system and suppressing the parasympathetic system. This leads to a variety of physiological changes, including an increased cardiac impulse, a rise in blood pressure, perspiration, muscle tone, and reduced activity of the stomach and intestines [23]. In this study, we employed physiological signals such as GSRs and electrocardiogram results to acquire information on actual changes in the subject.

5.2.4.1 Galvanic Skin Response

GSR is also called Electro-Dermal Activity (EDA). It has been used in studies on anxiety and stress and is cited as a method for detecting lies. The GSR is affected by the automatic nerve system, which can be divided into the sympathetic and parasympathetic systems in regard to stress responses. The main function of the sympathetic system is to stimulate physical activity to respond to stress, and if the automatic nerve system is facilitated, energy within the body is consumed and physical and mental stress occur. On the other hand, the main function of the parasympathetic system is to recover and conserve the energy of the body, making it deeply related to stress relief.

GSR differs according to human emotional changes, and increases according to the level of tension or excitement one experiences. Cognitive load theorists consider GSR as one way to measure cognitive load. Physiological signals such as the GSR do not require additional inquiry and observation, such as a questionnaire survey, and have the advantage of serving as objective measurement indicators. Ikehara and Crosby applied the GSR to measure cognitive load, and found that GSR varies depending on task difficulty [24]. Hypotheses regarding GSR and creativity activities are suggested as follows.

H1a: The rate of change in average GSR will affect exploration activity.
H1b: The rate of change in average GSR will affect exploitation activity.

5.2.4.2 Electrocardiogram

The automatic nerve system is evaluated by heart rate variability (HRV) through the use of an R-R electrocardiogram interval. HRV is an indicator of sympathetic and parasympathetic nerve activity and reflects changes in cardiac impulse. It can objectively and reliably evaluate automatic nerve adjustments in the heart and can also estimate the adjusting capacity of the human body, which represents the capability to counteract stress.

Electrocardiogram (ECG) is a signal reflecting the electrical activity of the heart, which pumps to circulate blood, and is indicated as a series of peaks that pertain to P-Q-R-S-T. As shown in Fig. 5.1, Peak R is the highest peak in both ways, and is repetitively indicated at every heartbeat. Generally speaking, a test on each ECG wave composed of P-Q-R-S-T is useful in diagnosing various heart diseases caused by organic lesions of the heart, whereas information on the R-R Interval among a series of Peaks R is useful in evaluating the function of the automatic nerve.

ECG is converted into an evaluation indicator (e.g., RMSSD, LF/HF Rate), where an analysis can be conveniently conducted through signal handling. As measured, ECG itself is the relative size of electrical signals indicated at the time of a cardiac impulse, and there are limitations in systematic and in-depth analyses. Accordingly, in order to analyze ECG data, it needs to be converted into an evaluation indicator such as heart rate (HR, beat/min) or standard deviation of normal to normal (SDNN) through signal handling [25].

In an HRV-based analysis, SDNN and RMSSD (square root of the mean of the sum of the squares of differences between adjacent R-R intervals) in the time domain and low frequency (LF; 0.04–0.15 Hz) and high frequency (HF; 0.15–0.4 Hz) in the

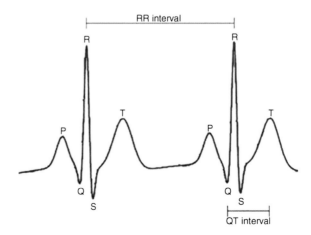

Fig. 5.1 R-R interval

frequency domain have been frequently used. The LF/HF ratio has generally been used in ECG analyses. The greater the workload, the higher the HR value compared to a recess, and SDNN increases compared to the baseline in situations involving stress [26]. The LF/HF ratio increases as the workload increases. Hypotheses regarding SDNN and creativity activities are suggested as follows.

H2a: The rate of change in SDNN will affect exploration activity.
H2b: The rate of change in SDNN will affect exploitation activity.

5.3   Research Design

In order to investigate how an individual conducts exploration and exploitation activities in various decision-making circumstances requiring creativity, an individual task-resolution circumstance was manipulated based on two factors and two levels as shown in Table 5.1. Physiological signals were measured to acquire the most objective results at the time of analysis. Individual decision-making circumstances were manipulated based on task difficulty and emotion. Task difficulty was divided into a difficult task and an easy task according to the level of a task that an individual needs to resolve, and emotion was classified into a case where an individual resolves a task with a positive emotion and that where emotion is not controlled.

5.3.1   Task

Participants performed a decision-making task through the use of the DSS. The task involved suggesting an alternative to resolving a problem through the use of the DSS Program and establishing a hierarchical criteria tree to select an alternative. The decision support software adopted for the test was Java Applet-based Web-HIPRE (HIerarchical PREference analysis in the World Wide Web, http://www.hipre.hut.fi/). The experiment was confined to suggesting alternatives and creating a criteria tree, which unveil the process and results of manifesting creativity to achieve the study objectives.

5.3.1.1   Task Difficulty

Two tasks, including a difficult task and an easy task, were prepared to investigate differences in the responses of test participants and the results of resolving tasks

Table 5.1 2×2 experiment design

Group	Difficulty task	Easy task
Positive emotion group	Group 1	Group 2
Control group	Group 3	Group 4

with different levels of difficulty. Graduate students and undergraduate students majoring in business were asked to list three to four difficult and easy tasks related to decision-making before other students were asked to select a task each considered easy or difficult from the list when thinking about selection criteria. This process was followed to select one difficult task and one easy task. Selecting a mobile phone was cited as a relatively easy task, and designating a radioactive nuclear waste disposal site was considered a difficult task.

5.3.1.2   Criteria Examples

When the subjects were resolving a task, as shown in Fig. 5.2, examples were suggested on the right side of the screen to objectively judge if the subjects resolved the task through an exploration or exploitation activity. Nine criteria that could help resolve the task were suggested, and some examples could be used as they were whereas others were not related to resolving the task. This means that test participants were allowed to creatively suggest selection criteria when resolving the task or choose some examples from the selection criteria given at the right hand side of the screen to constitute a tree.

5.3.1.3   Emotion Manipulation

Positive emotion was manipulated to see if there was any difference between a case where subjects resolved a task with positive emotion and a case where no positive

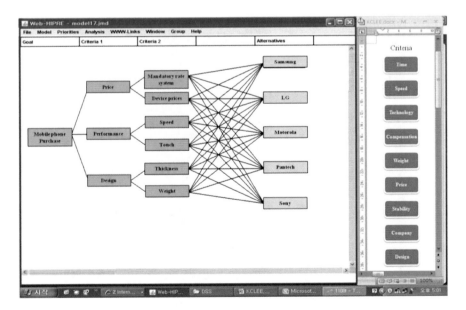

Fig. 5.2 Selection criteria tree through the use of Web-HIPRE (example)

emotion was involved. In order to manipulate the positive emotion, a small choco-
late bag with colorful packaging was given [27] or recent successes or events were
discussed with subjects [28]. For the manipulation of positive emotion, we selected
a method of engaging in discussions with subjects so they were reminded of fond
memories instead of receiving a present. The manipulation of emotion was intended
to give subjects in each of the two groups [28] a positive or negative emotion and a
case where the positive emotion was manipulated in only the experimental group
and the other group was considered a control group with no manipulation of emotion [27]. Positive emotion was manipulated in only one group, and the other group
did not go through any special manipulation. It stemmed from the judgment that if
a conversation that could generate a negative emotion stirs up unpleasant feelings,
determining to participate in a test would fail to generate appropriate results.

5.3.2 Apparatus

ECG and GSR are two signals used to measure physiological response in the process of resolving a task through the use of DSS. Based on Biopac MP150 System
(Biopac systems, CA, USA), ECG100C was used to measure ECG, and GSR100C
was used to measure GSR as shown in Fig. 5.3. Through the use of Biopac
AcqKnowledge Software (version 4.1), GSR100C Module and ECG100C Module
were attached to acquire GSR and ECG at the same time, as shown in Fig. 5.3. For
the setup of GSR100C, the gain was set at 10 Ω/v, low pass 1.0 Hz, high pass
0.05 Hz, and a sampling frequency of 125samples/s. ECG100C was sampled at
1,000 Hz and filtered from 0.5 to 35 Hz alone.

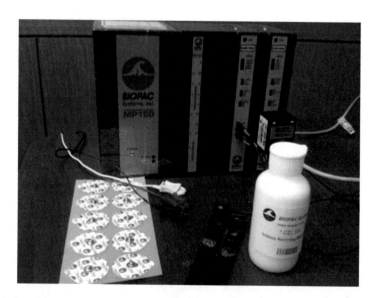

Fig. 5.3 Physiological signal measure equipment (GSR, ECG)

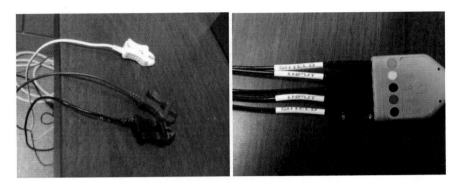

Fig. 5.4 ECG measure sensor

Electrodes were attached to the tip of the index and middle fingers of the subject's left hand to measure the GSR. The test required a mouse and a keyboard for the subject to establish a hierarchical criteria tree in DSS, but the left hand was used to acquire GSR data, so the work had to be done with the right hand. It was difficult to acquire ECG data through the limbs due to work done by the right hand, so the physiology signal was acquired through the chest. Three measuring tools were attached to the chest, with a red one attached to the left side of the chest, a white one attached to the right side of the chest, and a black one attached to the left side of the navel to acquire signals. Figure 5.4 shows ECG sensor used in this experiment.

5.3.3 Measurements

The variables included in the study were measured based on a multi-item scale following a 7-point Likert scale (1 strongly disagree, 7 strongly agree). The measurement items for each variable were modified and used to fit the study based on the measurement items whose reliability and validity had been supported in existing studies, as shown in Table 5.2. The operational definition was implemented by figuring out how the new selection criteria were used to resolve the task of exploration and how the existing selection criteria were used to resolve the task of exploration with regard to the exploitation variables [30–32].

5.4 Experiments

5.4.1 Participants

Forty-two healthy college students in their 20s participated in the study in order to increase accuracy and reduce errors. Participants were paid 20,000 won for their involvement in the study. The data analysis was based on 37 students because five

Table 5.2 Measurement items

Variable	Measurement items	References
Exploration	ER1 I aim to come up with new selection criteria to resolve a task.	Adapted from Lazer and Friedman [30], Prieto et al. [31], Song et al. [32]
	ER2 I've found new selection criteria to resolve a task.	
	ER3 I considered selection criteria from new perspectives to resolve a task.	
Exploitation	ET1 I mostly referred to existing selection criteria to resolve a task.	
	ET2 I frequently resolved a task by applying existing selection criteria.	
	ET3 I used known selection criteria to resolve a task.	

Table 5.3 Participants' demographics

Distinction		Frequency	Rate (%)
Gender	Male	20	54.1
	Female	17	45.9
	Total	37	100.0
Age	22 year and below	11	29.7
	23–25 years old	18	48.7
	26 year and above	8	21.6
	Total	37	100.0
Average hours of daily use of PC during the week	Less than 1 h	1	2.7
	1 h–less than 2 h	11	29.7
	2 h–less than 3 h	14	37.8
	3 h–less than 4 h	3	8.1
	4 h–less than 5 h	8	21.6
	Total	37	100.0

cases were excluded due to some students not understanding the task or the occurrence of data errors. Subject's demographics are shown in Table 5.3. About 78.4% of the participants were 25 years old or younger and 54% percent were male, with 46% female.

5.4.2 Procedure

The participants resolved the assigned task using Web-based decision-supported software, so the effect of the software needed to be controlled in the course of the test in order to acquire accurate test results. Toward this end, all subjects received software usage instruction and practice, in addition to decision-making education on selection criteria trees from a skilled experimental assistant in advance. The

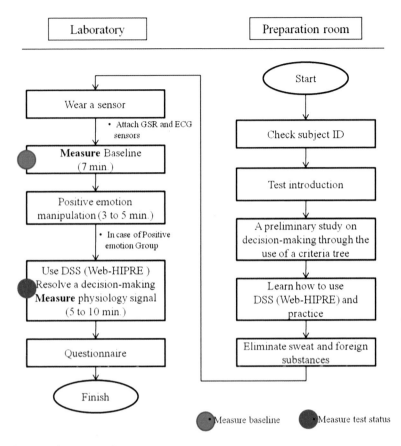

Fig. 5.5 Experiment procedures

experiment was conducted in two places, including a preparation room and a laboratory. Orientation was given in the preparation room, and equipment was set up in the laboratory before the measurement of physiological signals between the baseline and task-resolution states. Figure 5.5 is a diagram of the procedure used in the experiment.

5.4.2.1 Procedures in the Preparation Room

As the subject arrived to participate in the test, he or she was taken to a preparation room. The subject's name was checked to see if he or she was the right person, and a copy of an ID and a bankbook was received to pay the test participation fees. As the subjects needed to resolve a given task using Web-HIPRE DSS, explanations of decision-making based on a selection criteria tree were given prior to the test, and education on how to use the Web-HIPRE Program was offered along with practice.

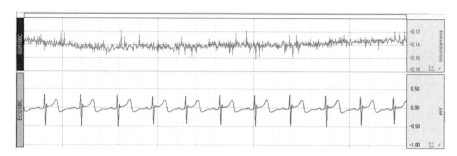

Fig. 5.6 Signals of GSR and ECG during meditation (example)

After practicing, the subjects needed to wash their hands before waiting to be called into the laboratory.

5.4.2.2 Procedures in the Laboratory

The subjects were first taken to a chair. Prior to the test, the subjects were asked to wash their hands, remove accessories (including rings and watches) from their left hand, and put away mobile phones in order to put on the experimental equipment. The subjects were asked to attach GSR measure equipment to the left hand using gel and ECG equipment was attached to the chest before checking the physiology signal input through the use of AcqKnowledge 4.1 Software. If there was no problem in inputting the physiology signal, the light was turned off for meditation for 7 min in order to acquire baseline data on GSR and ECG. Figure 5.6 is an illustration of the signal of GSR (red line) and ECG (blue line) during meditation.

In the manipulation of positive emotion, the interview aimed at eliciting a positive emotion was conducted for about 5 min. After meditation, the task directions and requirements were delivered. In the case of an easy task, participants were instructed to establish a decision-making tree on selecting a mobile phone, and were requested to suggest at least two phases for the depth of the tree and at least three alternatives for the mobile phone. For the difficult task, they were requested to establish a decision-making tree on the selection of a radioactive waste disposal site. In that case, participants were requested to suggest at least three phases for the depth of the tree and at least five alternatives. The subjects were asked to resolve the two tasks within 10 min and were asked not to use their left hand while working on the tasks. Figure 5.7 is an illustration of the signal of GSR (red line) and ECG (blue line) in the course of resolving a task.

The subjects were asked to remove the GSR and ECG equipment and complete a questionnaire after the activities. While the subjects completed the questionnaire, the GSR data acquired through Biopac were saved on a PC, and the decision-making tree and alternatives generated through the use of Web-HIPRE DSS were captured on the screen before being stored on the PC through the use of PowerPoint.

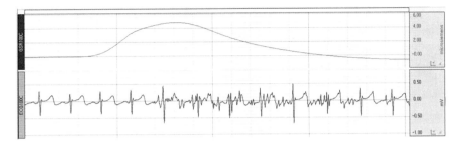

Fig. 5.7 Signals of GSR and ECG in the course of resolving a task (example)

Table 5.4 Manipulation check variable

Variable	Item	Cronbach's alpha
Task difficulty	1. The task itself was difficult.	0.968
	2. The task itself was not easy.	
Positive emotion	1. It was pleasant while a task was being resolved.	0.921
	2. A task was resolved with pleasure.	
	3. A task was resolved in a positive mood.	

5.5 Analysis

5.5.1 Manipulation Check

In considering the purpose of a test, task difficulty and positive emotion were operated at two levels, with variables measured on a 7-point Likert Scale through an after-the-fact questionnaire. The items used in the manipulation check are shown in Table 5.4.

Two types of tasks with different levels of task difficulty (easy, difficult) were suggested and a researcher assessed if the subjects recognized the task difficulty. The ANOVA results indicate that the manipulation of task difficulty was effective $(F(1,35)=33.890, p<0.000)$. The level of difficulty (mean=4.81) faced in resolving a task related to radioactive waste disposal sites was significantly higher than the level of difficulty (mean=2.32) participants experienced when resolving a task related to the selection of a mobile phone.

However, the manipulation check on positive emotional manipulation aimed to induce emotional changes among the sample when participating in tasks through ANOVA led to insignificant results $(F(1,35)=0.236, p=0.630)$. It is hard to tell whether discussing fond memories with subjects during a 5-min interview prior to resolving a task for the purpose of inducing a positive emotion continued during the process of resolving a task. Accordingly, as an alternative to ineffective emotional manipulation, we used the feelings that the subjects who completed the questionnaire for the manipulation check reported on resolving the task in order to analyze emotional changes. Although emotion was manipulated for the purpose of the study, it is actually the subject's emotion, so it is possible to conduct an analysis on the effect of psychological factors on exploration and exploitation activities based on emotional changes.

5.5.2 Physiological Signal Data Analysis

Regarding the data collected through the Biopac system, the GSR data were analyzed using AcqKnowledge (Version 4.1), an in-house analysis system, and the ECG data were analyzed using Kubios HRV analysis software (Version 2.0, Biomedical Signal and Medical Imaging Analysis Group, Department of Applied Physics, University of Kuopio, Finland) after converting them into RRI data. The indicator used to analyze the GSR data was average GSR. For the indicator used to analyze the ECG data, the time domain SDNN and frequency domain LF/HF ratio indicator were used to represent HRV. Generally speaking, a physiological signal needs to go through a normalization process to increase its analytical reliability due to individual differences [33, 34]. As there is no absolute normal value, an analysis needs to be conducted to assess changes compared to a stable state after normalization of test data measured during a stable state (baseline data) and during a stimulation state. Accordingly, the following formula was used to acquire a relative rate of change so that it could be used in the analysis. The average value of the GSR graph might be zero or less, so the rate of change before and after the fact was acquired through the use of (5.1), and the SDNN and LF/HF ratio calculated based on HRV was more than zero at all times, so the rate of change was acquired through the use of (5.2).

$$\text{Normalized Signal}(i) = \frac{\text{Signal}(i) - \text{Baseline}}{\text{Signal}_{max} - \text{Signal}_{min}} \times 100 \tag{5.1}$$

In (5.1), the maximum signal (Signal_{max}) and the minimum signal (Signal_{min}) are the greatest and smallest values in the entire status ranging from the baseline state to the test state. If (5.1) is used, it is converted to a value between 0 and 1.

$$\text{Normalized Signal}(i) = \frac{\text{Signal}(i) - \text{Baseline}}{\text{Baseline}} \times 100 \tag{5.2}$$

5.5.3 Results

The ANOVA results on the dependent variables—exploration and exploitation—through the use of physiological signals, average GSR and SDNN, the independent variables, showed that only the SDNN signal was significant. First, the rate of change in the average GSR registered by the subject while resolving the task did not significantly affect the creative activities: exploration (mean$_{decrease}$=4.72, mean$_{increase}$=4.54; p=0.728) and exploitation (mean$_{decrease}$=5.33, mean$_{increase}$=4.73; p=0.244). Thus, H1a and H1b are not supported. Second, the results show that the rate of change in SDNN significantly affects the creative activities, as hypothesized: exploration (mean$_{decrease}$=4.96, mean$_{increase}$=4.00; p<0.05) and exploitation (mean$_{decrease}$=4.44, mean$_{increase}$=5.28; p<0.10), thereby supporting H2a and H2b, respectively.

5.6 Discussion and Conclusion

The primary contribution of this study is examining the working mechanisms of creativity activities such as exploration and exploitation on individual levels based on physiological signal data. The results of the study led to several important findings. First, by explicitly manipulating the exploration and exploitation activities of participants when faced with different levels of task difficulty and emotion in a DSS environment, we gained a better understanding of the influence of an individual's stress level on creativity activities. Exploration activity was found to be facilitated in a less stressful environment, while exploitation occurred in the stressful situation, where an increasing rate of change in SDNN was considered to be a stressful situation [26], as shown in Fig. 5.8. An individual creativity manifestation process is expected to be facilitated and contribute to advancing corporate achievements by harmonizing the working environment for individuals in the corporate environment, which requires exploration or exploitation in order to compete. For example, in an environment that would benefit from exploration, providing an optimal environment where individuals can best exert creativity would lead to more effective results. If the environment makes individuals feel stressed or impatient, they are better off conducting exploitation activities than exploration activities, both psychologically and instinctively. Accordingly, if a business environment requires exploration, it would be helpful to create an environment where one feels relaxed and comfortable instead of an environment where one feels stressed and impatient.

Second, we measured physiological signals in the DSS environment aimed to resolve nonstructural problems that require creativity while examining the path (exploration, exploitation) where decision-makers exert creativity. As the results of studies exploring which behaviors induce creativity provide customized information on decision-makers' judgment, we can better understand how to develop a more effective DSS. Namely, as it perceives a decision-makers' physiology signal (context aware) and judges useful information that can help a decision-maker exert creativity—useful information for exploration or exploitation—before making a suggestion, it can improve the quality of decision-making. In a flood of information related to nondirectional decision-making, it can reduce decision-makers' options and facilitate the development of a system leading to effective decision-making.

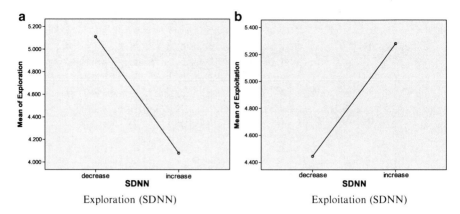

Exploration (SDNN)   Exploitation (SDNN)

Fig. 5.8 Results of SDNN on creativity activities. (**a**) Exploration (SDNN). (**b**) Exploitation (SDNN)

Finally, GSR and HRV are based on the automatic nerve system and reflect the physical state at the time of resolving a task. If data are analyzed through physiological signals in this way, information that is not gathered in self-reported questionnaires is expected to be extracted.

This study has the limitation that it could not appropriately control the subject's emotion at the time of resolving a task. One reason why emotional operation as applied in previous studies was not effective in the present study seems to be due to the fact that the subjects failed to maintain fond memories for the period of time prior to the initiation of the task, as they were preoccupied with the idea that they needed to generate a creative result within 10 min.

Acknowledgment This work was supported by the Korea Research Foundation Grant funded by the Korean Government (KRF-2009-342-B00015).

References

1. Amabile, T.M., Barsade, S.G., Mueller, J.S., Staw, B.M.: Affect and creativity at work. Adm. Sci. Q. **50**, 367–403 (2005)
2. Lee, K.C., Kwon, S.: An empirical study of individual digital creativity improvement mechanism in a working environment. Korean Manage. Rev. **38**, 457–481 (2009)
3. Hughes, G.D.: Add creativity to your decision processes. J. Qual. Participation. **52**, 5–13 (2003)
4. Forgionne, G., Newman, J.: An experiment on the effectiveness of creativity enhancing decision-making support systems. Decis. Support Syst. **42**, 2126–2136 (2007)
5. March, J.G.: Exploration and exploitation in organizational learning. Organ. Sci. **2**, 71–87 (1991)
6. George, J.M., Jing, Z.: Dual tuning in a supportive context: Joint contributions of positive mood, negative mood, and supervisory behaviors to employee creativity. Acad. Manage. J. **50**, 605–622 (2007)

7. Gilson, L.L., Mathieu, J.E., Shalley, C.E., Ruddy, T.M.: Creativity and standardization: Complementary or conflicting drivers of team effectiveness? Acad. Manage. J. **48**, 521–531 (2005)
8. Podsakoff, P.M., Organ, D.W.: Self-reports in organizational research: Problems and prospects. J. Manage. **12**, 69–82 (1986)
9. Amabile, T.M.: The social psychology of creativity: A componential conceptualization. J. Pers. Soc. Psychol. **45**, 357–376 (1983)
10. Weisberg, R.W.: Problem solving and creativity. In: Sternberg, R.J. (ed.) The Nature of Creativity: Contemporary Psychological Perspectives, pp. 148–176. Cambridge University Press, Cambridge (1988)
11. Simonton, D.K.: Origins of Genius: Darwinian Perspectives on Creativity. Oxford University Press, New York (1999)
12. Clore, G.L., Schwarz, N., Conway, M.: Cognitive causes and consequences of emotion. In: Wyer, R.S., Srull, T.K. (eds.) Handbook of Social Cognition, pp. 323–417. Lawrence Eribaum, Hillsdale, NJ (1994)
13. Frederickson, B.L.: What good are positive emotions? Rev. Gen. Psychol. **2**, 300–319 (1998)
14. Isen, A.: Positive affect. In: Dagleish, T., Power, M. (eds.) Handbook of Cognition and Emotion, pp. 521–539. Wiley, New York (1999)
15. Audia, P.G., Goncalo, J.A.: Past success and creativity over time: A study of inventors in the hard disk drive industry. Manage. Sci. **53**, 1–15 (2007)
16. Benner, M.J., Tushman, M.L.: Process management and technological innovation: A longitudinal study of the photography and paint industries. Adm. Sci. Q. **47**, 676–706 (2002)
17. Van Velsor, E., McCauley, C.D.: Our view of leadership development. In: McCauley, C.D., Velsor, E.V. (eds.) The Center for Creative Leadership: Handbook of Leadership Development, pp. 1–22. Jossey-Bass, San Francisco, CA (2004)
18. Malone, T.W., Lepper, M.R.: Making learning fun: A taxonomy of intrinsic motivations for learning. In: Snow, R.E., Farr, M.J. (eds.) Aptitude, Learning and Instruction. Lawrence Erlbaum Associates, Hillsdale, NJ (1987)
19. Candlin, C.: Towards task-based language learning. In: Candlin, C., Murphy, D. (eds.) Language Learning Tasks, pp. 5–22. Prentice-Hall, London (1987)
20. Skehan, P.: A framework for the implementation of task-based instruction. Appl. Linguist. **17**, 38–62 (1996)
21. Dawson, M.E., Schell, A.M., Fillon, D.L.: The Electrodermal System, Principles of Psychophysiology. Cambridge University Press, Cambridge, UK (1990)
22. Force, T.: Heart rate variability: Standards of measurement, physiological interpretation, and clinical use. Task Force of the European Society of Cardiology and the North American Society of Pacing and Electrophysiology. Circulation **93**(1043–1065) (1996)
23. Hancock, P.: Stress, Workload and Fatigue. Lawrence Erlbaum, Mahwah (2001)
24. Ikehara, C.S., Crosby, M.E.: Assessing cognitive load with physiological sensors. Paper presented at the 38th Hawaii International Conference on Systems Sciences, pp. 295–304. IEEE Computer Society, Big Island, Hawaii, USA (2005)
25. Berntson, G.G., Bigger Jr., J.T., Eckberg, D.L., Grossman, P., Kaufmann, P.G., Malik, M., Nagaraja, H.N., Porges, S.W., Saul, J.P., Stone, P.H., Van Der Molen, M.W.: Heart rate variability: Origins, methods, and interpretive caveats. Psychophysiology **34**, 623–648 (1997)
26. Salahuddin, L., Kim, D.: Detection of acute stress by heart rate variability using a prototype mobile ECG sensor. ICHIT '06: Proceedings of the 2006 International Conference on Hybrid Information Technology, pp. 453–459. IEEE Computer Society, Washington, DC, USA (2006)
27. Djamasbia, S., Stronga, D.M., Dishawb, M.: Affect and acceptance: Examining the effects of positive mood on the technology acceptance model. Decis. Support Syst. **48**, 383–394 (2010)
28. Anderson, C., Keltner, D., John, O.P.: Emotional convergence between people over time. J. Pers. Soc. Psychol. **84**, 1054–1068 (2003)
29. Tierney, P., Farmer, S.M., Graen, G.B.: An examination of leadership and employee creativity: The relevance of traits and relationships. Pers. Psychol. **52**, 591–620 (1999)

30. Lazer, D., Friedman, A.: The network structure of exploration and exploitation. Adm. Sci. Q. **52**, 667–694 (2007)
31. Prieto, I.M., Revilla, E., Rodriguez-Prado, B.: Managing the knowledge paradox in product development. J. Knowl. Manage. **13**, 157–170 (2009)
32. Song, S., Nerur, S., Teng, J.: An exploratory study on the roles of network structure and knowledge processing operation in work unit knowledge management. Database Adv. Inform. Syst. **38**, 8–26 (2007)
33. Lina, T., Morishimab, S., Maejimab, A., Tang, N.: The effects of virtual characters on audiences' movie experience. Interact. Comput. **22**, 218–229 (2010)
34. Prendinger, H., Ma, C., Ishizuka, M.: Eye movements as indices for the utility of life-like interface agents: A pilot study. Interact. Comput. **19**, 281–292 (2007)

Chapter 6
An Empirical Analysis of the Effect of Social and Emotional Intelligence on Individual Creativity Through Exploitation and Exploration

Min Hee Hahn, Do Young Choi, and Kun Chang Lee

6.1 Introduction

As the uncertainty of the global economy increased in the past few years, so did the need for creative problem solving among members of organizations in order to survive and grow. The creative big idea is becoming the center of the social change that leads to the development of businesses.

Since Guilford [21] stressed the importance of creativity in the American Psychology Association (APA), related research has been carried out using various approaches. Although there are minor differences in the definition of creativity among researchers, it is generally defined as the novel and useful production of ideas (Science Times, 2008). In the early days, research on creativity consisted of arguments asserting that personal characteristics and the environment could affect the frequency or level of creative behavior [4].

M.H. Hahn
SKK Business School, Sungkyunkwan University, Seoul 110-745, Republic of Korea
e-mail: minheehahn@gmail.com

D.Y. Choi
Solution Business Unit, LG CNS Co., Ltd, Seoul 100-725, Republic of Korea
e-mail: dychoi96@gmail.com

K.C. Lee (✉)
Department of Interaction Science, SKK Business School, Sungkyunkwan University, Seoul 110-745, Republic of South Korea
e-mail: kunchanglee@gmail.com

K.C. Lee (ed.), *Digital Creativity: Individuals, Groups, and Organizations*,
Integrated Series in Information Systems 32, DOI 10.1007/978-1-4614-5749-7_6,
© Springer Science+Business Media New York 2013

However, research on creativity has a deep relationship (both directly and indirectly) with paradigms such as psychology and pedagogy. Each scholar holds different perspectives on creativity, and many researchers have tried to provide a general framework for creativity by comparing and categorizing existing creativity research related to the various paradigms [25]. This means that creativity has to be interpreted as a multilateral phenomenon rather than as a single factor, and the integrated view that creativity is the result of cognitive, motivational, and environmental factors has recently gained strength and validity [4, 45].

The meaning and characteristics of creativity are becoming the core, essential condition for employees working in the radically changing IT environment because they must be sensitive to social change and are required to be in harmony with the times they are living in. Therefore, the IT industry is working to improve employees' harmonizing ability because social and human relationships are important qualities in this age requiring much cooperation and hugely diversified human networks.

For such reasons, the importance of social intelligence, which makes human relationships more flexible and improves job performance, is increasing, and researchers such as Goleman [20] have argued that complex "relationships" are very important in achieving social success. Goleman also argued that emotional intelligence and related practical and creative intelligence will lead the twenty-first century. As such, social and emotional intelligence are drawing attention as personal psychological characteristics among academics and in the business market.

In this research, we investigate how emotional and social intelligence, which can be used to successfully handle human relationships and can lead to harmonized human relationships in the existing social order, affect the creative process and individual creativity. We aim to show how social and emotional intelligence (the new paradigm as personal psychological variable factors) affect individual creativity. We study how exploration, or searching for new knowledge, and exploitation, or using existing knowledge, are related to personal psychological characteristics and individual creativity. In other words, we explore how emotional and social intelligence, which are personal psychological variables that strongly influence future society, affect the creative process and individual creativity of IT industry workers. Therefore, the purpose of this research can be summarized as follows.

First, we investigate the multidimensional relationship between social intelligence and emotional intelligence as psychological characteristics, exploitation and exploration as part of the creative process, and individual creativity. We also investigate hypotheses based on structural model verification, which describes how the variables are related to one another. Second, by conducting an empirical analysis on the relationship between the creative process, individual creativity, and the personal psychological characteristics for the improvement of individual creativity, we provide implications from both the academic and practical perspectives.

6.2   Literature Review

6.2.1   Social and Emotional Intelligence

6.2.1.1   Social Intelligence

Social intelligence is the ability to behave reasonably based on understanding the emotions, thoughts, and behaviors of ourselves and others in everyday life. In other words, social intelligence means being smart in relationships by being empathetic or having the ability to sense what others are feeling as well as their intentions. The discussion on social intelligence started when a psychologist, Thorndike [46], introduced the term "social intelligence" in Harpers Magazine at a time when the IQ test was drawing sensational interest as a tool for measuring an individual's intelligence. Research on this topic has been limited because the definition of such a concept has not been clearly made. However, Guilford [22] suggested that more research on the intellect model has been conducted in recent years. Goleman [20] recently defined social intelligence as the ability to positively and effectively lead relationships with others, making them harmonious and productive in the border of society.

Research on the multidimensional characteristics of social intelligence was first conducted in 1980 [20]. Wong et al. [49] discussed social perception, social insight, and social knowledge as components of social intelligence, and Jones and Day [27] discussed social perception, which refers to social clues, and social insight, which is the social behavior occurring in new situations, as two components of social intelligence.

Lee [31] distinguished social intelligence from creativity, which is not academic intelligence, to show that social intelligence exists as an independent concept. To prove the multidimensionality of social intelligence, he studied the relationship between social and cognitive flexibility and social knowledge, which are two basic social intelligence mechanisms. The research results showed that social intelligence and creativity are distinguishable, independent constructs. Flexibility with information use was found to be an important factor in solving social problems.

Various components of social intelligence mentioned in the theory of Thorndike [46] have recently been developed and include the study of consensus and interaction in society by Goleman [20]. Goleman divided social intelligence into social awareness (including empathy, attunement, empathic accuracy, and social cognition), which refers to feelings about other people, and social facility (including synchrony, self-presentation, influence, and concern), which is handling consciousness. Social awareness is a spectrum that encompasses feelings and understanding about other people's inner thoughts and emotions and joining the complex social circumstances. Social facility involves constructing smooth, effective interactions based on social awareness, so simply knowing another's thoughts and intentions cannot be said to be an effective interaction. In this research, we also measure social intelligence based on the research of Goleman.

6.2.1.2 Emotional Intelligence

Emotional intelligence has recently emerged as a topic of study among social and organizational psychologists (e.g., [35, 41]). The first researchers to use the concept of emotional intelligence were American psychologists Salovey and Mayer [40], whose work has received increasing attention since they defined emotional intelligence as "the subset of social intelligence that involves the ability to monitor one's own and others' feelings and emotions, to discriminate among them and to use this information to guide one's thinking and actions." Goleman later introduced the term "emotional intelligence" in *The Times* in 1995, and the term has since received a great amount of attention from researchers around the world [10].

Emotional intelligence is composed of cognitive and noncognitive aspects. In regard to the cognitive aspect, researchers such as Mayer and Salovey [35] defined emotional intelligence as intelligence that includes emotion and provided an emotional intelligence model composed of various emotional abilities. They also provided a psychometric method based on the model. The noncognitive aspect includes an individual's personal characteristics and focuses more on the function that handles and understands emotional information such as motivation [19]. Although the latter concept of emotional intelligence became more popular than the psychometric method, it overlaps with the components of character and suffers from the criticism that it lacks objectivity because it does not provide a method for measuring the suggested components.

Until now, it could be said that research related to emotional intelligence has been composed of research designed to derive academic agreement at the concept level. This research has been based on a definite interpretation of individual emotional intelligence by many researchers, pivoting on Goleman [19] and following the definition of emotional intelligence by Salovey and Mayer [40] as the ability to recognize and control one's own and others' emotions.

Among various academics who have contributed to the development of the emotional intelligence construct, two groups of scholars have been of prime importance: Davies et al. [13] and Salovey and Mayer [40]. In 1998, Davies et al. [13] qualitatively summarized the emotional intelligence literature and developed a four-dimensional definition of emotional intelligence. However, they did not develop a measure of emotional intelligence, instead using earlier work on emotional intelligence and a group of emotional intelligence-related measures to show that they loaded on the same factors as the Big Five personality dimensions. On the basis of these cross-loadings in a series of exploratory factors analyses, Davies et al. [13] concluded that emotional intelligence is an elusive construct.

In response to the findings of Davies et al. [13], Wong and Law [50] developed a new emotional intelligence scale (the Wong and Law Emotional Intelligence Scale, or WLEIS) using the four-dimensional definition of emotional intelligence introduced by Davies et al. [13]. Wong and Law [50] insisted that emotional intelligence is composed of the ability to clearly understand and express self-emotion (*Self-Emotions Appraisal (SEA)*), the ability to recognize and understand the emotions of others (*Others-Emotions Appraisal (OEA)*), the ability to use the emotional information that an individual has to achieve greater performance (*Use of Emotion (UOE)*), and the ability to control personal emotions in accordance with the given situation (*Regulation of Emotion (ROE)*). They found that a leader's emotional intelligence affects the job satisfaction and organizational behavior of subordinates, and the subordinates' emotional intelligence also affects their job performance and job satisfaction in the research utilizing a self-administered questionnaire survey composed of self-developed WLEIS. The sample included 149 pairs of Hong Kong University's leaders and subordinates and 146 Hong Kong government administrators. In this research, we measured emotional intelligence using the results of Wong and Law [50].

6.2.2   Exploitation and Exploration

The concepts of exploitation and exploration were first introduced by March [34] and are currently regarded as important mechanisms in the growth and survival of an organization. Exploitation is explained by terms such as refinement, choice, production, efficiency, selection, implementation, and execution, while exploration can be explained by terms such as search, variation, risk-taking, experimentation, play, flexibility, discovery, and innovation. Exploitation minimizes change and focuses on efficiency, whereas exploration is change-pursuing, risk-taking, and experiment-oriented [34]. Levinthal and March [33] defined exploration as "the pursuit of new knowledge, of things that might come to be known" and exploitation as "the use and development of things already known." In this study, we adopted these definitions of exploitation and exploration.

The returns on exploitation are definite and obtained in a short period of time. In contrast, the returns on exploration are indefinite, requiring a considerable amount of time and having pervasive effects [34]. The results from exploitation bring more definite, instant returns and at the same time bring the discovery of new solutions. However, in the long run, it could bring obsolescence [24]. In contrast, although exploration enables the discovery of new solutions, the pursuit of these solutions often fails and therefore could lead to a decrease in short-term performance. After all, exploitation produces more definite, instant returns and exploration creates and preserves essential knowledge for maintaining long-term organizational learning [33].

It is very challenging to carry out exploration and exploitation activities at the same time [33, 34] because exploration and exploitation activities have the tendency to exclude each other. In other words, the delicate trade-off characteristics when allocating resources between the exploration of emerging technologies and exploitation of existing knowledge have made these a central research topic in research on adaption and survival as well as research on innovation and organizational learning. On the other hand, March [34] stated that exploration and exploitation are the two extremes in one dimension, and in such a context, the research on organizational learning points out that maximizing these two in one organization is not a simple task [32–34]. In other words, when focusing on the exploration of new capabilities, the speed of improving existing capabilities decreases, whereas in the case of focusing only on the exploitation of existing capabilities, it becomes difficult to create new capabilities to deal with radical environmental changes.

Therefore, it is meaningful to view exploitation and exploration as independent constructs, but taking a view on the interrelationship between the two also has significant benefits. In the IT industry, a large number of projects are carried out, and depending on the characteristics of the project there are cases where fast learning is required, cases where exploration through slow learning is more important, and in most cases, both are required. In such a context, this research is carried out in empirical studies that include workers actually working in the IT industry.

Many researchers have studied exploration–exploitation from various perspectives. For example, some researchers have applied these constructs to strategic alliances, product development, and organizational innovation and performance [23]. Most existing research explains exploration and exploitation as independent variables or dependent variables. For instance, Nerkar [36] investigated the impacts of temporal exploitation and exploration on later knowledge creation, and Benner and Tushman [8] studied the influence of process management on exploitative and explorative innovations.

In this study, we do not try to put out comprehensive interpretations about exploitation and exploration, but focus on the perspective of balancing exploration and exploitation to improve individual creativity. Previous studies indicate that maintaining an appropriate balance between exploration and exploitation activities is a primary factor in a firm's survival and prosperity [34].

6.2.3 Individual Creativity

Guilford [21] stated that creativity is a continuous trait in all people and that individuals with recognized creative talent simply have "more of what all of us have" [21], and since then research on creativity has been carried out in various fields with a focus on creativity among individuals [2], work groups [29, 38], and entire organizations [51]. There are various theories on creativity and the approaches and methods also vary. In addition, each method has unique characteristics, and therefore, it is difficult to make one unified definition. The concept of creativity is being applied to art, science, literature, business, and other areas [47], which leads to various views on creativity. In other words, creativity is a complex concept that has been defined by many researchers [42]. Although the terminologies used by researchers differ, all of them deal with similar concepts. The most recent general definition is explained as a concept that includes "the generation of novel behavior that meets a standard of quality or utility" (e.g., [15]). Creativity is the production of novel and useful ideas (or products; e.g., [2, 4, 37]).

The history of creativity research, which started with the speech of Guilford [21], the father of creativity studies, at an American Psychology Association (APA) meeting can be categorized according to different time periods: basic research on creativity in the 1950–1960s, research on the individual difference variables and learning program in the 1970–1980s, and lastly, research based on the ecological approach as the dimensional perspective that stresses interactions among the creativity component factors from the 1990s to the present [25].

Since the 1990s, more research on individual creativity has been carried out in the field of management, with two main streams of research. The first includes research focused only on the independent variables that affect creativity and the second is focused on the moderating variables. Research focused only on the independent variables is composed of three parts. First is the study of the personal characteristics that affect creativity, including intelligence [7], cognitive style [2], and personality [48]. Second are the research studies investigating the contextual characteristics that affect creativity, such as leadership [44], organizational support [3], downsizing [1], the creative atmosphere of the organization [17], rewards [14], and expectations of coworkers regarding this type of research. Last is research addressing the interactions among personal and contextual characteristics, with active research in this area (e.g., [37]). Previous research on individual creativity has mainly focused on personal and contextual characteristics and their interactions.

6.3   Research Model and Hypotheses

Exploitation and exploration have been discussed as part of the process leading to creative or innovative performance [5]. Researchers have also suggested that social and emotional intelligence are important factors that affect creativity [20]. With this phenomenon, we know that emotional intelligence, which represents the harmony of human relationships through the understanding and sympathy in today's organized society [19], and social intelligence, which is the index that measures creative intelligence in handling and solving problems of meaning and values and that must be developed in the process of self-realization [20], are essential and important qualities within the personal and psychological characteristics of workers in the IT industry, for whom creative talent is required.

For the research analysis, we investigate how emotional and social intelligence, which are personal psychological characteristics, affect the creative process and individual creativity. We also explore ways in which the creative process influences individual creativity. Based on previous studies, we set the research model (Fig. 6.1) as below.

6.3.1   Personal Psychological Characteristics and Creativity

Based on are view of many previous studies, the common point of today's successful people is that their social intelligence is high. In fact, to increase efficiency through

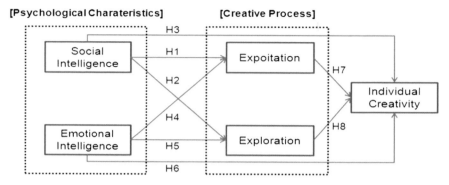

Fig. 6.1 Individual creativity model

cooperation, it is necessary to read other people's emotions by understanding the situation and making quick decisions in social networks such as the amplectant cobweb [20]. Another reason why social intelligence is regarded as the most important ability factor in the future is that cooperation is very important in the community.

According to the research of Barchard [6], social intelligence is composed of the skills that create useful social products and is an important factor in solving social problems. In addition, Goleman [20] viewed satisfaction and a sense of responsibility as strong indicators of creative intelligence in dealing with the meaning and value of problems as well as their solutions. After all, individuals with high social intelligence can understand and control the emotions of other people relatively well and improve the performance of an organization through harmonization. Therefore, we propose the following hypotheses in our investigation of the relationship between social intelligence and individual creativity based on the discussion of Goleman [20], who argued that social intelligence leads to an increase in an individual's creativity index and an improvement in job performance.

Hypothesis 1: Social intelligence positively influences exploitation.

Hypothesis 2: Social intelligence positively influences exploration.

Hypothesis 3: Social intelligence positively influences individual creativity.

Isen [26] studied the relationship between laughing and problems that require creative solutions. He found that stronger emotion takes place when individuals face a problematic situation, and this emotion leads the individual's attention to the new problem. Therefore, when people pay attention to their own emotions, rather than interrupting the currently underway cognitive activities, emotion helps them to internally decide the order of priority and allocate the surrounding resources according to that order.

Cooper and Sawaf [12] argued that individuals can be the most creative when they are energetic and pleasant with ample emotion. Similarly, Goleman [19] discussed emotional intelligence and emotional competency, arguing that learned emotional competency, which improves performance based on emotional intelligence, is two times as important as cognitive ability in predicting staff members' creative performance. Lastly, Fabio [16] found that leaders with the highest performance cause more than three times the amount of laughter than leaders with average performance. This indicates that a more positive atmosphere leads individuals to accept information more effectively and helps them react more sensibly and creatively. Previous studies show that people's emotions affect their thoughts and behavior, and that they solve problems more actively with creative behavior in a positive emotion situation. Therefore, taking into account the results of preceding researchers, we derived the following research hypotheses.

Hypothesis 4: Emotional intelligence positively influences exploitation.

Hypothesis 5: Emotional intelligence positively influences exploration.

Hypothesis 6: Emotional intelligence positively influences individual creativity.

6.3.2   Creative Process and Individual Creativity

Exploitation takes advantage of existing knowledge and resources, facilitating the utilization of existing knowledge and resources [11]. The exploration capability allows members to develop more innovative solutions for tricky problems [28]. In other words, exploitation seeks a differentiated solution from the existing solution by using existing knowledge, while exploration is carried out as an innovative activity. A new solution is found in such a process and new knowledge is gained through the learning process [34]. Audia and Goncalo [5] divided creativity into two concepts: divergent creativity and incremental creativity. They explained divergent creativity and incremental creativity in relation to exploration and exploitation, respectively.

It is natural to assume that exploration and exploitation activities are related to creative activities as well as individual creativity. The theory of exploration–exploitation is potentially useful for understanding the creative process because it incorporates past success as a factor impacting the propensity to explore new ideas [5]. Therefore, we propose the following research hypotheses.

Hypothesis 7: Exploitation positively influences individual creativity.

Hypothesis 8: Exploration positively influences individual creativity.

6.4 Experiment and Results

6.4.1 Measurement of Constructs

One of the characteristics of people with high social intelligence is that they regard themselves with a positive attitude and have a strong sense of responsibility. They are tolerant to other people, enjoy cooperation, and have high satisfaction with the organization's cooperative achievement [20]. Goleman and Boyatzis [18] found that there is a large difference in the level of achievement between leaders with high and low levels of social intelligence. In this research, we operationally defined social intelligence as "the ability to lead harmonious human relationships and to solve the problems in effective and creative ways." In addition, we used the items focused on the "Social Intelligence and the Biology of Leadership" provided in the research of Goleman and Boyatzis [18].

We made the operational definition of emotional intelligence "the ability to recognize other people's emotion, effectively control and manage the emotion." Wong and Law [50] developed the Wong and Law Emotional Intelligence Scale (WLEIS), a self-administered questionnaire survey for which empirical studies of many businesses or organizations are possible. WLEIS is a very simple but trustworthy measurement tool that can be applied to the research of Law et al. [30] for its validity and reliability. Therefore, we used WLEIS, the verified measurement tool of Law et al. [30], to measure emotional intelligence.

We followed the definition of Levinthal and March [33] of exploration and exploitation as the creative process. They defined exploration as "the pursuit of new knowledge, of things that might come to be known" and exploitation as "the use and development of things already known." To measure these variables, we used the survey items verified by Prieto et al. [39] and Song et al. [43].

Finally, we used the verified creativity survey items from the research of Zhou and George [52] to measure individual creativity. They studied the relationship between job dissatisfaction and employees creativity, and in the final analysis, employees' creativity was found to be the highest when continuance commitment was high. Creativity was found to be manifested when there was useful feedback from coworkers, a coworker provided help and support, or perceived organizational support for creativity was high.

In this research, we used survey items that have been verified in previous studies. In the process, we changed a few terms and carried out the survey in Korean, which is our native language, for consideration of the survey targets' type of business. The measurement items of each variable were modified based on the reliability and validity of items found in previous studies. The variables included in this study were measured based on a multi-item scale following a 7-point Likert Scale format (1 strongly disagree, 7 strongly agree). In Table 6.1, the questions used for the measurement and the related research are shown.

Table 6.1 Measures and items

Constructs		Measurement items	References
Social intelligence		Do you persuade others by engaging them in discussion and appealing to their self-interests?	Goleman and Boyatzis [18]
		Do you get support from key people?	
		Do you coach and mentor others with compassion and personally invest time and energy in mentoring?	
		Do you provide feedback that people find helpful for their professional development?	
		Do you provide a fascinating vision, build group pride, and encourage people to have a positive emotion?	
		Do you lead by bringing out the best in people?	
		Do you require input from everyone on the team?	
Emotional intelligence	Self-emotions appraisal (SEA)	I have a good sense of why I have certain feelings most of the time.	Wong and Law [50]
		I have good understanding of my own emotions.	
		I really understand what I feel.	
		I always know whether I am happy.	
	Others-emotions appraisal (OEA)	I always know my friends' emotions from their behavior.	
		I am a good observer of others' emotions.	
		I am sensitive to the feelings and emotions of others.	
		I have good understanding of the emotions of people around me.	
	Use of emotion (UOE)	I always set goals for myself and then try my best to achieve them.	
		I always tell myself I am a competent person.	
		I am a self-motivating person.	
		I would always encourage myself to try my best.	
	Regulation of emotion (ROE)	I am able to control my temper so that I can handle difficulties rationally.	
		I am quite capable of controlling my own emotions.	
		I can always calm down quickly when I am very angry.	
		I have good control of my own emotions.	

(continued)

Table 6.1 (continued)

Constructs	Measurement items	References
Exploitation	I combine the existing valuable knowledge elements for carrying out the task.	Prieto et al. [39]
	I carry out the task by applying the existing competences related to products/services that are currently being offered.	
	I work by combining new and existing ways of doing things without stifling their efficiency.	
	I apply the lessons learned in other areas of the organization in the task.	Song et al. [43]
	I carry out the task by using the in-company output (knowledge management system, etc.).	
	I work by utilizing the past experiences (including myself and other colleagues).	
Exploration	I am well-motivated to improve the field with which I was dissatisfied in the past.	Prieto et al. [39]
	I will create the new solution about the field with which I was dissatisfied in the past.	
	I utilize the new knowledge and method in carrying out the task.	
	From carrying out the task, the new and utilizable knowledge and outputs are produced.	
Individual creativity	I suggest new ways to achieve goals or objectives.	Zhou and George [52]
	I comes up with new and practical ideas to improve performance.	
	I searches out new technologies, processes, techniques, and/or product ideas.	
	I am a good source of creative quality.	
	I am a risk taker.	
	I promotes and stimulate other people's idea.	
	I exhibit creativity in the task whenever the opportunity comes.	
	I develops adequate plans and schedules for the implementation of new ideas.	
	I often come up with new and innovative ideas.	
	I deal with creative solutions to problems.	
	I often take a fresh approach to problems.	
	I suggests new ways of performing work tasks.	

6.5   Data Collection

For the empirical analysis, we selected staff members who consult and respond to customers in the Korean IT industry as the target group for the analysis. This group was judged to be very suitable for the analysis of the relationship between social intelligence, emotional intelligence, exploitation, and exploration because they work in an actual business. The target of the survey was limited to IT consulting, IT Planning, R&D Researcher, System Analyst, Requirement, Analyst and IT Analyst because these employees are those whose tasks must be met in various forms such as idea sharing, discussions, and brainstorming through smooth communication with the related departments, and they must produce creative output through cooperation.

In September 2011, the online survey was carried out over a period of 1 week. Surveys with errors or missing responses were excluded from the analysis, leaving a total of 447 respondents included in the present analysis. The characteristics of these respondents are shown in Table 6.2.

All of the respondents are employed in a job that requires the ability to find new solutions and use existing knowledge by understanding and fulfilling the requirements of customers.

Table 6.2 Characteristics of respondents

Category		No.	Portion (%)
Gender	Male	368	82.3
	Female	79	17.7
Age	19–29	88	19.7
	30–39	276	61.7
	40–49	72	16.1
	50–59	11	2.5
Position	Junior	196	43.8
	Advisory	190	42.5
	Senior	61	13.6
Work experience	~5 year	180	40.3
	5–10 year	127	28.4
	10–15 year	93	20.8
	15 year and above	47	10.5
Job type	IT consulting	112	25.1
	IT planning	99	22.1
	R&D research	97	21.7
	System analysis	58	13.0
	Requirement analysis	41	9.2
	IT analysis	40	8.9
Total		447	100.0

6.5.1 Reliability and Construct Validity

To analyze the theoretical research model and our own research hypotheses, we used SmartPLS 2.0, a type of partial least squares (PLS) software. PLS is a structural equation modeling tool that uses a component-based approach for estimation, so it places minimal restrictions on the sample size and residual distribution [9]. Therefore, PLS is especially useful in areas where there is weak theory and limited understanding of the relationships between variables. PLS has its own strength in that it can evaluate the structural and measurement models at the same time. Therefore, PLS analysis, which focuses on causal prediction, is more suitable than other SEM techniques, which attach greater importance to model fitness.

We conducted reliability and validity analyses to examine whether the questionnaire items matched our intent. The items were first tested for scale reliability. The Cronbach's alpha scores all exceeded 0.7, indicating high internal consistency. The convergent validity was assessed by reviewing the t-test for factor loading. The convergent and discriminant validity were also assessed by examining the composite reliability and average variance extracted (AVE; see Table 6.3).

As we can see from the factor loading scores presented in Table 6.1, all scores are above 0.5, indicating that the measurement items do a good job in explaining the constructs. The composite reliability and AVE measures exceed the threshold of 0.7 and 0.5, respectively, and therefore, we can conclude that the convergent validity of the measurement model is reasonable.

The discriminant validity of the instrument was assessed by examining the correlations among the questions. For discriminant validity, a measure should correlate with all measures of the same construct more highly than it does with any measures of other constructs. For satisfactory discriminant validity, the AVE from the construct should be greater than the variance shared between the construct and other constructs in the model. Table 6.4 presents the correlation matrix with correlations among the constructs and the square root of AVE on the diagonal. As shown in Table 6.4, the analysis of the discriminant validity showed that it was at an acceptable level.

6.5.2 Hypothesis Testing and Interpretation

The results of the analysis of the causality in the SEM are shown in Fig. 6.2.

The interpretation of the PLS results is based on the R^2 values of the dependent variable, which is explained by the independent variables as well as through the path coefficient's size, sign, and statistical significance. In this model, the R^2 values of all constructs are above the 10% recommended value. These results provide strong support for the posited relationships among the constructs. The R^2 value of individual creativity, which is the last dependent variable explained by the independent variables, is 69.2%, with R^2 values of 55.9% for exploitation and 47.7% for exploration. Table 6.5 summarizes the results regarding the research hypotheses.

Table 6.3 Reliability and convergent validity

Construct		Measurement item	Factor loading	Cronbach's α	Composite reliability	AVE
Social intelligence		SQ1	0.550	0.850	0.887	0.529
		SQ2	0.627			
		SQ3	0.713			
		SQ4	0.644			
		SQ5	0.691			
		SQ6	0.716			
		SQ7	0.617			
Emotional intelligence	Self-emotions appraisal (SEA)	EQ_SEA1	0.749	0.919	0.930	0.526
		EQ_SEA2	0.809			
		EQ_SEA3	0.792			
		EQ_SEA4	0.549			
	Others-emotions appraisal (OEA)	EQ_OEA1	0.644			
		EQ_OEA2	0.807			
		EQ_OEA3	0.815			
		EQ_OEA4	0.747			
	Use of emotion (UOE)	EQ_UOE1	0.733			
		EQ_UOE2	0.781			
		EQ_UOE3	0.774			
		EQ_UOE4	0.746			
	Regulation of emotion (ROE)	EQ_ROE1	0.723			
		EQ_ROE2	0.796			
		EQ_ROE3	0.830			
		EQ_ROE4	0.863			
Exploitation		ET1	0.771	0.866	0.901	0.602
		ET2	0.804			
		ET3	0.632			
		ET4	0.588			
		ET5	0.640			
		ET6	0.715			
Exploration		ER1	0.719	0.871	0.912	0.722
		ER2	0.716			
		ER3	0.653			
		ER4	0.607			
Individual creativity		IC1	0.578	0.936	0.946	0.597
		IC2	0.592			
		IC3	0.560			
		IC4	0.663			
		IC5	0.650			
		IC6	0.589			
		IC7	0.710			
		IC8	0.699			
		IC9	0.735			
		IC10	0.792			
		IC11	0.765			
		IC12	0.758			

Note: The construct which is composed of second order factor such emotional intelligence are analyzed by directly connecting all indicators used in first order factor to second order factor

Table 6.4 Discriminant validity

Construct	EQ	ER	ET	IC	SQ
EQ	**0.726**				
ER	0.646	**0.850**			
ET	0.725	0.699	**0.776**		
IC	0.718	0.747	0.632	**0.773**	
SQ	0.705	0.629	0.641	0.720	**0.728**

Note: The bold phase values of the correlation is the square root value of AVE.

SQ: social intelligence, *EQ:* emotional intelligence, *ET:* exploitation, *ER:* exploration, *IC:* individual creativity

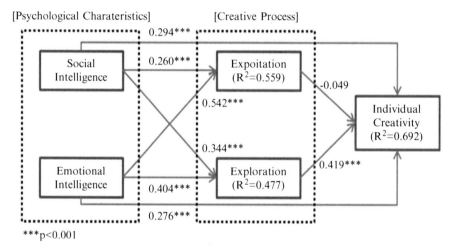

Fig. 6.2 Research model results. ***$p < 0.001$

Table 6.5 Results of hypotheses testing

H-No.	Path name	Path coefficient	t-value	Result
H1	SQ --> ET	0.260	4.697***	Accept
H2	SQ --> ER	0.344	5.451***	Accept
H3	SQ --> IC	0.294	6.538***	Accept
H4	EQ --> ET	0.542	9.914***	Accept
H5	EQ --> ER	0.404	6.813***	Accept
H6	EQ --> IC	0.276	5.696***	Accept
H7	ET --> IC	−0.049	0.964	Reject
H8	ER --> IC	0.419	9.204***	Accept

***$p < 0.001$

Based on the validity tests, all hypotheses except H7 were statistically significant and therefore were accepted. The interpretation of the test results for each hypothesis is as follows. First, H1 and H2, which argue that social intelligence positively affects exploitation and exploration, respectively, were accepted at a 99.9% confidence level and the path coefficients were 0.260 and 0.344, respectively.

This indicates that social intelligence positively affects exploitation, which involves using existing resources and knowledge, and exploration, which involves adding new resources and exploring new knowledge in a work environment that requires creativity, especially in customer service jobs such as those held by the sample in this study.

Second, H4 and H5, which posit that emotional intelligence has positive relationships with exploitation and exploration, respectively, were accepted at a 99.9% confidence level, with path coefficients of 0.542 and 0.404, respectively. This means that, in the relationship between exploration, exploitation, and social intelligence, individuals with higher emotional intelligence are more capable of exploitation and exploration.

Third, H7 (exploitation positively affects individual creativity) was rejected, while H8, which states that exploration positively affects individual creativity, was accepted with a 99.9% confidence level and the path coefficient was 0.419. This suggests that simply using existing knowledge does not directly affect individual creativity. Only when the activity is done to seek and explore new knowledge will individual creativity be directly affected.

Lastly, H3 and H6, which state that social intelligence and emotional intelligence directly affect individual creativity, respectively, were accepted at a 99.9% confidence level and the path coefficients were 0.294 and 0.276, respectively. In other words, individuals with high social and emotional intelligence, which are personal psychological characteristics, utilize existing knowledge and explore new knowledge relatively well. However, at the same time, we could not find a directly significant effect on individual creativity.

6.6 Discussion and Conclusion

In this research, we proposed a new research model of individual creativity from the perspectives of the creative process and personal psychological characteristics. An empirical analysis was conducted, with the sample including staff working in the IT industry, an area in which individual creative activities are vigorously undertaken. The results show that personal psychological characteristics, measured by social and emotional intelligence, have significant effects on the creative process and individual creativity. Exploration, which does not utilize existing knowledge, was found to significantly affect individual creativity, while exploitation was not found to directly strengthen individual creativity.

This could be treated as a very meaningful result in the sense that the creative process and individual creativity are strengthened as social and emotional intelligence are strengthened. In other words, from the perspective of an organization, carrying out personal education and creating a suitable atmosphere for each individual may increase the creativity of each member. Below is a discussion on the directions that the creative process, social intelligence, and emotional intelligence must have.

First, higher social intelligence and personal psychological characteristics are associated with stronger individual creativity. A common characteristic of today's successful people is high social intelligence. Developing one's social intelligence in order to read the emotions of other people in the social relations network can be helpful and may also increase creativity, which is one of the most important ability factors. Second, higher emotional intelligence is associated with improved creative processes and individual creativity. This leads us to deduce that the ability to motivate or encourage employees to do their best is related to individual creativity. Therefore, for excellent job performance, an individual should find a method to improve his individual creativity by understanding and controlling his own and coworkers' emotions, cultivating the ability to use such emotions and encourage self-motivation by setting goals. Third, exploration has a more direct effect on individual creativity than exploitation when viewed from the perspective of the creative process. Therefore, from the organization's point of view, helping utilize existing knowledge and creating an environment in which individuals can engage in exploration are very important.

In this research, we investigated how personal psychological characteristics and the creative process can be used to increase individual creativity for both individuals and businesses. The results are based on an empirical study in a business environment for which creativity is very important. As with any study, we must consider the limitations and future research issues. First, this research cannot be applied to employees in all industries because only employees in the IT industry were included in the present study. Therefore, in future research, we can expand the study to explore if there are differences in the relationship between personal psychological characteristics and creativity in other industries. A second limitation of this research is that social and emotional intelligence were the only factors considered to affect individual creativity. Therefore, a more systematic explanation could be given if other personal psychological characteristics are considered in future research. Third, we did not include environmental characteristics, which can also affect individual creativity. Individual creativity is affected by various factors in addition to personal psychological factors. Therefore, the inclusion of environmental characteristics in future studies could provide more meaningful results.

Acknowledgment   This work was supported by the Korea Research Foundation Grant funded by the Korean Government (KRF-2009-342-B00015).

References

1. Amabile, T.M., Conti, R.: Changes in the work environment for creativity during downsizing. Acad. Manage. J. **42**, 630–640 (1999)
2. Amabile, T.M.: Creativity in Context; Update to The Social Psychology of Creativity. WestView, Boulder, CO (1996)
3. Amabile, T.M.: Motivating creativity in organizations: On doing what you love and loving what you do. Calif. Manage. Rev. **40**(1), 39–58 (1997)

4. Amabile, T.M.: The social psychology of creativity: A componential conceptualization. J. Pers. Soc. Psychol. **45**, 357–376 (1983)
5. Audia, P.G., Goncalo, J.A.: Past success and creativity over time: A study of inventors in the hard disk drice industry. Manage. Sci. **52**(1), 1–15 (2007)
6. Barchard, K.A.: Emotional and social intelligence: Examining its place in the nomological network. Unpublished Doctoral Dissertation, University of British Columbia (2001)
7. Barron, F., Harrington, D.M.: Creativity, intelligence, and personality. Annu. Rev. Psychol. **32**, 439–476 (1981)
8. Benner, M.J., Tushman, M.L.: Process management and technological innovation: A longitudinal study of the photography and paint industries. Adm. Sci. Q. **47**, 676–706 (2002)
9. Chin, W.W.: The partial least squares approach to structural equation modeling. In: Marcoulides, G.A. (ed.) Modern Methods for Business Research, pp. 295–336. Lawrence Erlbaum Associates, NJ (1998)
10. Ciarrochi, J., Forgas, J., Mayer, J. (eds.): Emotional Intelligence in Everyday Life: A Scientific Inquiry, vol. 1, pp. 157–188. Psychology Press/Taylor & Francis, Philadelphia, PA (2001)
11. Cohen, W.M., Levinthal, D.A.: Absorptive capacity: A new perspective on learning and innovation. Adm. Sci. Q. **35**, 128–152 (1990)
12. Cooper, R.K., Sawaf, A.: Executive EQ: Emotional Intelligence in Leadership and Organizations, vol. 7, pp. 81–94. Gosset/Putnam, New York (1997)
13. Davies, M., Stankov, L., Roberts, R.D.: Emotional intelligence: In search of an elusive construct. J. Pers. Soc. Psychol. **75**, 989–1015 (1998)
14. Eisenberger, R., Armeli, S., Pretz, J.: Can the promise of reward increase creativity? J. Pers. Soc. Psychol. **74**, 704–714 (1998)
15. Eisenberger, R., Haskins, F., Gambleton, P.: Promised reward and creativity: Effects of prior experience. J. Exp. Soc. Psychol. **35**, 308–325 (1999)
16. Fabio, S.: Leadership in education: Effective UK college principals. Nonprofit Manag. Leadersh. **14**, 171–189 (2003)
17. Gilson, L.L., Shalley, C.E.: What leaders need to know: A review of social and contextual factors that can foster or hinder creativity. Leadership Quart. **15**, 33–53 (2004)
18. Goleman, D., Boyatzis, R.: Social intelligence and the biology of leadership. Harv. Bus. Rev. **86**(9), 74–81 (2008)
19. Goleman, D.: Emotional Intelligence. Bantam Books, New York (1995)
20. Goleman, D.: Social Intelligence: The New Science of Human Relationships. Bantam Books, New York (2006)
21. Guilford, J.P.: Creativity. Am. Psychol. **5**, 444–454 (1950)
22. Guilford, J.P.: The Nature of Human Intelligence. McGraw-Hill, New York (1967)
23. He, Z.L., Wong, P.K.: Exploration vs exploitation: An empirical test of the ambidexterity hypothesis. Organ. Sci. **15**, 81–94 (2004)
24. Holland, J.: Genetic algorithms. Sci. Am. **267**, 66–72 (1992)
25. Isaksen, S.G., Murdock, M.C.: The emergence of a discipline: Issues and approaches to the study of creativity. In: Isaksen, S.G., Murdock, M.C., Firestien, R.L., Treffinger, D.J. (eds.) Understanding and Recognizing Creativity: The Emergence of a Discipline, pp. 13–47. Ablex, Norwood, NJ (1993)
26. Isen, A.M., Daubman, K.A., Nowicki, G.P.: Positive affect facilitates creative problem solving. J. Pers. Soc. Psychol. **52**, 122–131 (1987)
27. Jones, K.L., Day, J.: Discrimination of two aspects of cognitive social intelligence from academic intelligence. J. Educ. Psychol. **89**, 486–497 (1997)
28. Katila, R., Ahuja, G.: Something old, something new: A longitudinal study of search behavior and new product introduction. Acad. Manage. J. **45**, 1183–1194 (2002)
29. Kurtzberg, T., Amabile, T.M.: From Guilford to creative synergy: Opening the black box of team-level creativity. Creativity Res. J. **13**, 285–294 (2001)
30. Law, K., Wong, C., Song, J.: The construct and criterion validity of emotional intelligence and its potential utility for managements studies. J. Appl. Psychol. **89**, 438–496 (2004)

31. Lee, J.E.: Social intelligence: Flexibility and complexity and distinct from creativity. Unpublished Doctoral Dissertation, University of Notre Dame (1999)
32. Levinthal, D.A.: Organizational adaptation and environmental selection-interrelated processes of change. Organ. Sci. **2**, 141–145 (1991)
33. Levinthal, D.A., March, J.G.: The myopia of learning. Strateg. Manage. J. **14**, 95–112 (1993)
34. March, J.G.: Exploration and exploitation in organizational learning. Organ. Sci. **2**, 71–87 (1991)
35. Mayer, J.D., Salovey, P.: What is emotional intelligence? In: Salovey, P., Sluyter, D. (eds.) Emotional Development and Emotional Intelligence: Educational Implications, pp. 3–34. Basic Books, New York (1997)
36. Nerkar, A.: Old is good? The value of temporal exploration in the creation of new knowledge. Manage. Sci. **49**, 211–229 (2003)
37. Oldham, G.R., Cummings, A.: Employee creativity: Personal and contextual factors at work. Acad. Manage. J. **39**(3), 607–634 (1996)
38. Paulus, P.B., Larey, T.S., Dzindolet, M.T.: Creativity in groups and teams. In: Turner, M.E. (ed.) Groups at Work: Theory and Research. (Applied Social Research Series), pp. 319–338. Lawrence Erlbaum Associates, Inc, Mahwah, NJ (2001)
39. Prieto, I.M., Revilla, E., Rodrýʹguez-Prado, B.: Managing the knowledge paradox in product development. J. Knowl. Manage. **13**, 157–170 (2009)
40. Salovey, P., Mayer, J.D.: Emotional intelligence. Imagin. Cognit. Pers. **9**, 185–211 (1990)
41. Schutte, N.S., Malouff, J.M., Bobik, C., Coston, T.D., Greeson, C., Jedlicka, C., et al.: Emotional intelligence and interpersonal relations. J. Soc. Psychol. **141**, 523–536 (2001)
42. Shalley, C.E., Gilson, L., Blum, T.C.: Matching creativity requirements and the work environment: Effects on satisfaction and intentions to leave. Acad. Manage. J. **43**, 215–223 (2000)
43. Song, S., Nerur, S., Teng, J.: An exploratory study on the roles of network structure and knowledge processing orientation in the work unit knowledge management. Adv. Inf. Syst. **38**, 8–26 (2007)
44. Sosik, J.J., Kahai, S.S., Avolio, B.J.: Leadership style, anonymity, and creativity in group decision support systems: The mediating role of optimal flow. J. Creative Behav. **33**, 227–256 (1999)
45. Sternberg, R.J., Lubart, T.I.: An investment theory of creativity and its development. Hum. Dev. **34**, 1–32 (1991)
46. Thorndike, E.L.: Intelligence and its uses. Harpers Magazine. **140**, 227–235 (1920)
47. Williams, W.M., Yang, L.T.: Organizational creativity. In: Sternberg, R.J. (ed.) Handbook of Creativity, pp. 373–391. Cambridge University Press, Cambridge, England (1999)
48. Wolfradt, U., Pretz, J.: Individual differences in creativity: Personality, story writing, and hobbies. Eur. J. Pers. **15**, 297–310 (2001)
49. Wong, C.M.T., Day, J.D., Maxwell, S.E., Meara, N.M.: A multitrait-multimethod study of academic and social intelligence in college students. J. Educ. Psychol. **87**, 117–133 (1995)
50. Wong, C.S., Law, K.S.: The effects of leader and follower emotional intelligence on performance and attitude: An exploratory study. Leadership Quart. **13**, 243–274 (2002)
51. Woodman, R.W., Sawyer, J.E., Griffin, R.W.: Toward a theory of organizational creativity. Acad. Manage. Rev. **18**, 293–321 (1993)
52. Zhou, J., George, J.M.: When job dissatisfaction leads to creativity: Encouraging the expression of voice. Acad. Manage. J. **44**, 682–696 (2001)

Chapter 7
Scenario-Based Management of Team Creativity in Sensitivity Contexts: An Approach with a General Bayesian Network

Do Young Choi, Kun Chang Lee, and Young Wook Seo

7.1 Introduction

The concept of creativity spans a multitude of domains, from art to science, to literature, to business and beyond [28]. In recent years, great attention has been paid to team creativity, rather than to individual creativity, because most management activities are conducted in team contexts. Organizations have typically thought of teams as the primary means of harnessing the creativity necessary to remain vital and effective [16]. This research focuses on the perceptions of team creativity and asks two questions: How do the processes of creative revelation — exploitation and exploration — engaged in by team members contribute to building team creativity, and how do environmental factors — organizational learning culture, knowledge sharing, and expertise heterogeneity — affect team creativity? As teamwork becomes an increasingly important part of organizations, it is critically important for managers and scholars to better understand the detailed processes through which team creativity is created.

D.Y. Choi
LG CNS Co. Ltd., Seoul 100-725, Republic of Korea
e-mail: dychoi96@gmail.com

K.C. Lee (✉)
Department of Interaction Science, SKK Business School,
Sungkyunkwan University, Seoul 110-745, Republic of South Korea
e-mail: kunchanglee@gmail.com

Y.W. Seo
Software Engineering Center at National IT Industry Promotion Agency,
Seoul 138-711, Republic of Korea
e-mail: seoyy123@gmail.com

K.C. Lee (ed.), *Digital Creativity: Individuals, Groups, and Organizations*,
Integrated Series in Information Systems 32, DOI 10.1007/978-1-4614-5749-7_7,
© Springer Science+Business Media New York 2013
99

Regression methods are typically applied to research on team creativity. However, rigid functional forms of regression methods may limit the interpretability of the analyses. To overcome such rigidness, this research proposes a new approach: the General Bayesian Network (GBN). The GBN is unique because its structure addresses the causal relationships between all variables. Moreover, researchers can simulate and experiment with the variables using such varied techniques as what-if and goal-seeking analysis. Through methods like this, they can draw significant conclusions. We adopt the GBN to induce a causal relationship among the six variables on which our research focuses: team creativity, exploitation, exploration, organizational learning culture, knowledge sharing, and expertise heterogeneity.

7.2 Previous Studies

7.2.1 Team Creativity

Though creativity has been defined in a variety of ways by researchers in different fields, it can be considered as the ability to produce something new and innovative [1]. Previous studies on the factors that affect creativity have extended the level of analysis from individuals to teams and organizations [9, 29]. Several researchers have stressed that team creativity depends on the nature of interactions among team members and on the social environment, both of which encourage innovation within organizations [14, 15]. Of the factors that influence team creativity, we have chosen five on which to focus from two perspectives: team creativity revelation processes and environmental factors. By focusing on team members' exploitation and exploration, as well as environmental factors like organizational learning culture, knowledge sharing, and expertise heterogeneity, we can gain a richer understanding of how team creativity is induced in organizational working environments.

Regarding the team creativity revelation processes, we can adopt the concept of exploitation and exploration as defined by Lazer and Friedman [10]. While exploitation can be defined as the process that enhances a team's capability by utilizing known knowledge and known solutions, exploration can be defined as the process that creates new capabilities by developing unknown knowledge and unknown solutions. In the perspective of innovation and creativity, exploitation and exploration have been regarded as the important processes [25]. Many studies of innovation stressed that generation of new ideas and creation of new knowledge are the critical factors in the component of innovation [18, 25]. In addition, creativity is regarded as the most essential factor of innovation processes [2, 27].

Regarding environmental factors that influence team creativity, many researchers have stressed organizational learning culture, knowledge sharing, and expertise heterogeneity. Considering the studies of Senge [23] and Garvin [5], we can infer that teams with positive organizational learning culture can expedite their creativity. Also knowledge sharing is a significant factor affecting team creativity. Knowledge sharing can be defined as interactions among team members for acquiring knowledge within an organization [21]. Knowledge sharing can improve a team's productivity as well as its capability for problem solving [17]. In order to address expertise heterogeneity, Tiwana and Mclean [26] define it as the diversity in the expertise possessed by the members. When teams have various members who have different knowledge, skills, and capabilities, they can enhance their capabilities, performances, and eventually creativity [19].

7.2.2 Bayesian Network

A Bayesian network (BN) consists of a set of nodes and a set of directed arcs. Each node represents a probability distribution that may, in principle, be continuous or discrete. However, in this paper, the formulation is restricted to the discrete case in which each node represents a finite set of states where each state is associated with a probability measure. Arcs indicate conditional probabilistic dependence so that the probability of a dependent variable being in a particular state is given for each combination of the states of the preceding variables. The dependence structure is thus represented by a set of conditional probability distributions. BN is referred to as directed acyclic graphs (DAG), indicating that loops (or cycles) are not allowed.

To each variable A with parents $pa(A)$, a conditional probability table $P[A|pa(A)]$ is attached. By using the conditional probability table (CPT), BN specifies a unique joint probability distribution $P(U)$ given by the product of all CPTs specified in BN: Let BN be a BN over $U = \{A_1,...,A_n\}$. Then $P(U) = \prod_{i=1}^{n} P[A_i | pa(A_i)]$

A BN can be used as a reasoning tool under uncertainty, meaning that decision makers facing uncertainty are able to rely on a BN to get robust decision support about the target problem. Especially, a BN is an excellent mechanism for updating a prior belief. For example, decision makers usually have a prior belief about some variables of interest. However, when additional information about the variables concerned is available, such an initial belief should be updated to represent recently available information.

From the structural point of view, the most general type of BN is a GBN [3, 4, 12, 22]. In comparison with a Naïve Bayesian Network (NBN) and Tree Augmented Naïve Bayesian Network (TAN), a GBN is very flexible in formulating its structure. Given a class node (or target node), a set of relevant explanatory nodes can be linked together [22]. Therefore, if decision makers seek a set of valid causal relationships between the class node and related variables, then the GBN seems a very effective BN model.

In the past, BNs have been applied to a wide range of problems. Early applications include medical diagnosis based on observation of symptoms, e.g., the pathfinder system of Heckerman et al. [7] has over 100 nodes. However, there are few studies adopting the general causal relationships supported by the GBN to solve creativity management problems like in our study.

7.3   Research Methodology and Experiment

7.3.1   Questionnaire and Survey

To analyze the relationships among factors affecting team creativity, measurement items for survey research were adapted and redeveloped from reliable literature and measured on a 7-point, Likert-type scale. Table 7.1 summarizes the questions used for the survey and the related researchers. For example, in the case of team creativity, survey items were adapted from Gibson and Vermeulen [6]. Exploitation and exploration were measured by six measurement items that were adapted from the studies of Lee and Choi [11], Katila and Ahuja [8], and Prieto et al. [20]. In order to measure organizational learning culture, knowledge sharing, and expertise heterogeneity, measurement items were developed from the previous studies based on Marsick and Watkins [13], Staples and Webster [24], Tiwana et al. [26], and Pelled et al. [19].

After building the questionnaire, a professional research firm was commissioned to survey. The firm randomly selected the proposal teams of system integration companies in South Korea. We received 222 responses (44 teams) from the research firm and after an assessment of the response quality, 211 responses (43 teams) were selected as suitable for this study. The demographic characteristics are summarized in Table 7.2.

7.3.2   Reliability and Confirmatory Factor Analysis

Six constructs were used in the research question: team creativity, exploitation, exploration, organizational learning culture, knowledge sharing, and expertise heterogeneity. As shown in Table 7.3, Cronbach's alpha values for the six constructs were all greater than 0.7, indicating that these items were reliable. In addition, principal component analysis with the varimax rotation option was used to test the validity of each item. The first factor, exploitation, explained 32.96% of the total variance, and the second factor, organizational learning culture, 17.56%. The total variance explained by the six factors was 83.35%. On the basis of these results, we concluded that the measurement items were statistically valid.

7.3.3   Experiment Results

To apply the GBN mechanism to the questionnaire data, we calculated the average values for each factor and then transformed the Likert scale for each factor into either Low (1–3) or Medium (3–5) or High (5–7). Causal relationships among the six variables are depicted by the GBN results in Fig. 7.1.

Table 7.1 Measures and items

Construct	Measurement items	References
Team creativity	Our proposal team creates new ideas about how to perform tasks.	Gibson and Vermeulen [3]
	When new method is introduced, that method comes from our proposal team.	
	Our proposal team creates sometimes new ideas which other proposal teams refer to.	
Exploitation	I combine the existing valuable knowledge elements for carrying out the task.	Lee and Choi [11] Katila and Ahuja [8] Prieto et al. [20]
	I carry out the task by applying the existing competences related to products/services that are currently being offered.	
	I work by combining new and existing ways of doing things without stifling their efficiency.	
	I apply the lessons learned in other areas of the organization in the task.	
	I carry out the task by using the in-company output (knowledge management system, etc.).	
	I work by utilizing the past experiences (including myself and other colleagues).	
Exploration	I am well-motivated to improve the field with which I was dissatisfied in the past.	Prieto et al. [20]
	I will create the new solution about the field with which I was dissatisfied in the past.	
	I utilize the new knowledge and method in carrying out the task.	
	From carrying out the task, the new and utilizable knowledge and outputs are produced.	

(continued)

Table 7.1 (continued)

Construct	Measurement items	References
Organizational learning culture	Employees of my company obtain compensations for learning activities.	Marsick and Watkins [13]
	Employees of my company spend their times to build up trust each other.	Staples and Webster [24]
	Employees of my company update their ideas and knowledge by group discussion or information gathered.	Tiwana et al. [26]
	Employees of my company use lessons learned.	Pelled et al. [19]
	My company recognized the employees who create new ideas.	
	My company work together with external expertise groups in order to meet my company's needs.	
	Leaders of my company search continuously opportunities.	
Knowledge sharing	I can access information related proposal tasks with organizational approach.	
	Members outside proposal team willingly share their knowledge, information, and experiences with our proposal team members.	
	I easily perform my proposal tasks by using knowledge already exists in my company.	
	I make use of standardized documents in order to share and deliver knowledge related to proposal tasks.	
Expertise heterogeneity	Members of our proposal team are much different in their expertise knowledge area.	
	Members of our proposal team have different background and experiences.	
	Technology and capability which members of our proposal team hold are complementary each other.	

Table 7.2 Demographic characteristics of respondents

Category		No.	Percentage (%)
Gender	Male	185	87.7
	Female	23	10.9
	N/A	3	1.4
Age	20–29	28	13.3
	30–39	100	47.4
	40–49	70	33.2
	50 and above	8	3.8
	N/A	5	2.4
Work experience	Less than 5 year	52	24.6
	5–10 year	49	23.2
	10–15 year	61	28.9
	15–20 year	25	11.8
	More than 20 year	24	11.4
Job level	Junior	72	34.1
	Advisory	102	48.3
	Senior	25	11.8
	Executive	8	3.8
	N/A	4	1.9

Table 7.3 Reliability and factor analysis ($n = 43$ teams)

Variables	Item	Cronbach's alpha	ET	OLC	TC	KS	EH	ER
Exploitation	ET2	0.886	0.899	0.091	−0.064	0.030	0.190	0.200
	ET1		0.879	−0.024	0.143	0.053	0.195	0.154
	ET3		0.798	0.346	0.108	−0.102	−0.027	0.218
	ET4		0.737	0.236	0.017	0.257	0.207	−0.260
Organizational	OLC2	0.876	0.105	0.866	0.266	−0.082	0.066	0.006
learning	OLC1		0.091	0.833	0.083	0.052	0.008	0.383
culture	OLC3		0.382	0.805	0.288	−0.046	−0.057	0.124
Team creativity	TC2	0.876	0.069	0.236	0.899	0.166	0.093	−0.023
	TC1		0.012	0.200	0.872	0.100	−0.137	0.204
Knowledge	KS2	0.716	0.040	0.066	0.173	0.824	0.153	−0.120
sharing	KS1		0.059	−0.003	−0.040	0.774	−0.131	0.019
	KS3		0.017	−0.181	0.134	0.750	0.347	−0.100
Expertise	EH1	0.800	0.141	−0.134	−0.045	0.231	0.904	0.103
heterogeneity	EH2		0.434	0.254	0.043	−0.027	0.787	−0.012
Exploration	ER2	0.760	0.177	0.236	0.095	−0.129	0.024	0.898
	ER1		0.231	0.240	0.525	−0.098	0.176	0.588
Variance explained (%)			32.957	17.556	13.507	7.544	6.324	5.459
Total variance explained (%)			32.957	50.512	64.020	71.564	77.888	83.347

ET exploitation, *OLC* organizational learning culture, *TC* team creativity, *KS* knowledge sharing, *EH* expertise heterogeneity, *ER* exploration

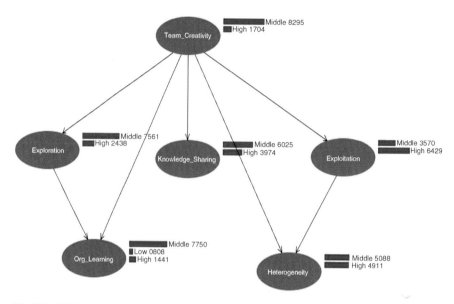

Fig. 7.1 GBN with team creativity as a target node

First, five variables of exploitation, exploration, organizational learning culture, knowledge sharing, and expertise heterogeneity were found to have a direct relationship to team creativity. Second, exploration is related to organizational learning culture. Likewise, exploitation is associated with expertise heterogeneity. The prediction accuracy of this model was 86.05%. Consequently, casual relationships are able to be easily identified using GBN.

In order to find out how the posterior probabilities of each variable would change, we simulated three scenarios based on our team creativity model with the what-if and goal-seeking capability of GBN.

Scenario 1-1 (What-if analysis: the effect of environmental factors): Among explanatory variables, if each value of the environmental factors is high respectively (i.e., a value between 5 and 7) and no other variables are changed, how do the team creativity and other variables change?

As shown in Fig. 7.2a, an organizational learning culture is directly related to team creativity and exploration. Originally, the prior probability of middle team creativity has the largest probability. However, if the value of organizational learning is set to be high, the posterior probability of the high team creativity becomes the largest. Based on this result, we can infer that an increase in the value of the organizational learning culture helps increase a team's creativity level. In addition, the value of exploration changes the most favorably when the value of the organizational learning culture increases.

Regarding the causal relationship of knowledge sharing (refer to Fig. 7.2b), it relates directly only to team creativity. Though the posterior probability of the middle

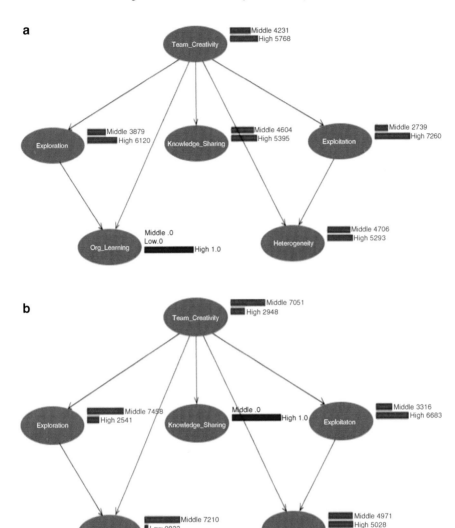

Fig. 7.2 What-if analysis result: environmental factors. (**a**) High value of organizational learning culture. (**b**) High value of knowledge sharing

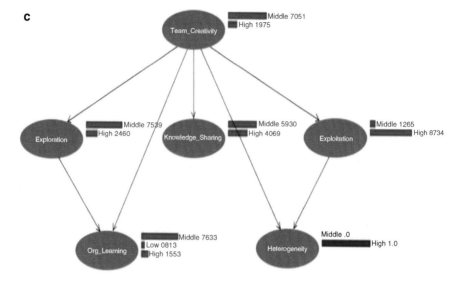

Fig. 7.2 (continued) (**c**) High value of expertise heterogeneity

team creativity remains largest when the value of knowledge sharing is set to be high, the value of team creativity changes favorably. Expertise heterogeneity relates directly to team creativity and exploitation as shown in Fig. 7.2c. The value of team creativity also changes favorably as in the case of knowledge sharing. Also, the value of exploitation changes the most favorably when the value of the expertise heterogeneity increases.

Scenario 1-2 (What-if analysis: the effect of creativity revelation processes): Among explanatory variables, if each value of the creativity revelation processes— exploitation and exploration—is high (i.e., a value between 5 and 7) and no other variables are changed, how do the team creativity and other variables change?

Figure 7.3 shows the results of the posterior probability when the value of exploitation and that of exploration are set to be high. Exploitation has direct relationships with team creativity and knowledge heterogeneity. The target variable—team creativity— changes favorably and the posterior probability for the high level of expert heterogeneity increases the most as shown in Fig. 7.3a. Exploration relates directly to team creativity and organizational learning culture. When the value of exploration is set to be high, the value of team creativity changes favorably and the high level of organizational learning culture becomes the largest as shown in Fig. 7.3b.

Scenario 2 (Goal-seeking analysis): For team creativity to be high, what other factors should be changed?

Consequently, a team's creativity is affected directly or indirectly by five variables: exploitation, exploration, organizational learning culture, knowledge sharing,

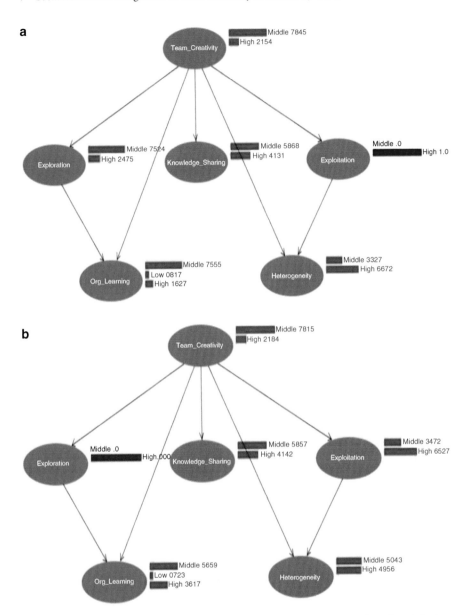

Fig. 7.3 What-if analysis result: creativity revelation process. (**a**) High value of exploitation.
(**b**) High value of exploration

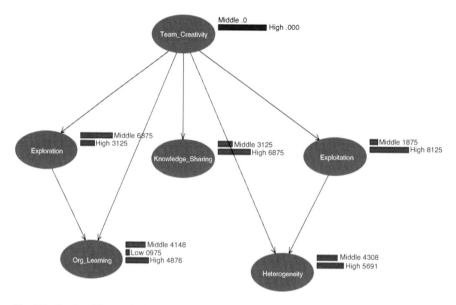

Fig. 7.4 Goal-seeking analysis result

and expertise heterogeneity. When the team's creativity is set to the highest level, the posterior probability for each high level of all of the variables increases. Among these variables, the levels of two variables—organizational learning culture and knowledge sharing—increased the most when the value of team creativity is set to be high as shown in Fig. 7.4. Therefore, we can find that organizational learning culture and knowledge sharing can have the most effect on increasing a team's creativity.

7.3.4 Discussion

From the analysis of the GBN results, it was found that those factors on which this research focuses—exploitation, exploration, organizational learning culture, knowledge sharing, and expertise heterogeneity—directly affect a team's creativity. In addition, we found a causal relationship among these variables. That is, exploration is related to organizational learning culture, and exploitation is associated with expertise heterogeneity. We also found that the most important variable affecting a team's creativity is the organizational learning culture. Through the causal relationship and several scenario experiments (what-if and goal-seeking analysis), we found several implications for managers to effectively manage a team's creativity.

First, in the perspective of creativity revelation processes, both exploitation and exploration are important processes for enhancing a team's creativity. Specifically, exploitation is more closely associated with expertise heterogeneity and exploration has stronger relationship with organizational learning culture. When we consider the concept and characteristics of exploitation and exploration, the meaning of these relationships becomes clear. As exploitation can be defined as the process that enhances a team's capability by utilizing known knowledge and known solutions [10], those teams that consist of diverse members with various expertise, knowledge, skills, and backgrounds can enhance the teams' problem-solving capability through exploitation processes with existing knowledge and solutions that team members hold by active interactions. Therefore, we can infer that exploitation has a strong relationship with expertise heterogeneity and those factors can affect a team's creativity at the same time as shown in the results of this research. Furthermore, when we consider exploration as developing a capability for unknown knowledge and unknown solutions [10], those teams with a high level of organizational learning culture can enhance the exploration capability of the teams and consequently the level of the team's creativity can increase. Therefore, in a practical sense, not only should managers encourage team members to pursue exploitation and exploration, they should build a working environment in which team members can learn each other's expertise and voluntarily learn new knowledge in the context of organizational learning.

Second, the GBN results show that environmental factors—organizational learning culture, knowledge sharing, and expertise heterogeneity—directly affect a team's creativity. Therefore, managers should consider creating an organizational learning culture in a creative environment and should build a knowledge-sharing atmosphere through the vitalization of several organizational mechanisms such as Knowledge Management System (KMS) or knowledge award programs, etc. Also, managers should consider that their teams are designed to have various expertise among team members.

Third, the importance of an organizational learning culture and knowledge sharing was confirmed because it is the most seemingly influential factor on for a team's creativity as shown in our scenario-based experiments. Therefore, an organizational learning culture and knowledge sharing should be handled by team managers for effective team creativity management.

Finally, managers can do relevant simulations with various scenarios as in this research. This research proved that GBN can be an appropriate method for managing factors that affect a team's creativity.

7.4 Concluding Remarks

Organizations have focused on increasing their responsiveness and ability to foster innovation. They should be concerned not only with fostering creativity and innovation among individual employees, but also with developing creative and innovative teams. However, few studies have investigated the relationship between team creativity and individual creativity. Moreover, few studies have tried to analyze the causal relationships among factors that affect a team's creativity or to propose practical guidelines for teams that are trying to come up with more effective creativity management strategies. We proposed useful management methods for improving a team's creativity by performing a variety of scenario-based sensitivity analyses based on the GBN. The findings we obtained using the GBN are as follows: First, we found that team creativity is closely related to exploitation, exploration, organizational learning culture, knowledge sharing, and expertise heterogeneity. Second, exploration is associated with organizational learning culture, and exploitation is related to expertise heterogeneity. Third, using scenario-based simulations, we found that an organizational learning culture and knowledge sharing should remain high to sustain high levels of team creativity. To the best of our knowledge, this study is the first attempt to apply the GBN to the research question: Why do exploration, exploitation, and environmental factors affect a team's creativity? Our experiences with the GBN convinced us that the GBN has great potential to identify causal relationships and to conduct sensitivity analyses. Nevertheless, our research has limitations. First, we considered only five variables. Other control variables, such as task complexity and team size, as well as other team-related factors, need to be introduced. Second, our research targeted members of proposal teams who worked together for short periods of time in system integration companies. Therefore, our results may be difficult to generalize to entire organizations.

Acknowledgment This work was supported by the Korea Research Foundation Grant funded by the Korean Government (KRF-2009-342-B00015). This study was also partially supported by WCU (World Class University) program through the National Research Foundation of Korea funded by the Ministry of Education, Science and Technology (Grant No. R31-2008-000-10062-0).

References

1. Amabile, T.M.: A model of creativity and innovation in organizations. In: Staw, B.M., Cummings, L.L. (eds.) Research in Organizational Behavior, vol. 10, pp. 123–167. JAI Press, Greenwich (1988)
2. Amabile, T.M.: Creativity in Context. Westview, Boulder, CO (1996)
3. Cheng, J., Greiner, R.: Learning Bayesian belief network classifiers: Algorithms and system. In: 14th Canadian Conference on Artificial Intelligence, June 7-9, pp. 141–151 (2001)
4. Friedman, N., Geiger, D., Goldszmidt, M.: Bayesian network classifiers. Mach. Learn. **29**, 131–163 (1997)
5. Garvin, D.A.: Building a learning organization. Harv. Bus. Rev. **71**, 78–91 (1993)
6. Gibson, C., Vermeulen, F.: A healthy divide: Subgroups as a stimulus for team learning behavior. Adm. Sci. Q. **48**(2), 202–239 (2003)
7. Heckerman, D., Horvitz, E., Nathwani, B.: Toward normative expert systems: Part 1. The pathfinder project. Methods Inf. Med. **31**, 90–105 (1992)
8. Katila, R., Ahuja, G.: Something old, something new: A longitudinal study of search behaviour and new product introduction. Acad. Manage. J. **45**, 1183–1194 (2002)
9. Kurtzberg, T.R., Amabile, T.M.: From Guilford to creative synergy: Opening the balck box of team-level creativity. Creativity Res. J. **13**, 285–294 (2001)
10. Lazer, D., Friedman, A.: The network structure of exploration and exploitation. Adm. Sci. Q. **52**, 667–694 (2007)

11. Lee, H., Choi, B.: Knowledge management enablers, processes, and organizational performance: An integrative view and empirical examination. J. Manage. Inform. Syst. **20**, 179–228 (2003)
12. Madden, M.G.: On the classification performance of TAN and general Bayesian networks. Knowl. Based Syst. **22**, 489–495 (2009)
13. Marsick, V.J., Watkins, K.E.: Demonstrating the value of an organization's learning culture: The dimensions of the learning organization questionnaire. Adv. Dev. Hum. Res. **5**(2), 132–151 (2003)
14. Mednick, S.: The associative bias of the creative process. Psychol. Rev. **69**, 220–232 (1962)
15. Milgram, R.M., Rabkin, L.: Developmental test of Mednick's associative hierarchies of original thinking. Dev. Psychol. **16**, 157–158 (1980)
16. Mohrman, S.A., Cohen, S.G., Mohrman, A.M.: Designing Team Based Organizations. Jossey-Bass, New York (1995)
17. Nelson, K.M., Cooprider, J.G.: The contribution of shared knowledge to IS group performance. MIS Quart. **20**(4), 409–432 (1996)
18. Nijstad, B.A., De Dreu, G.K.W.: Creativity and group innovation. Appl. Psychol. Int. Rev. **51**, 400–406 (2002)
19. Pelled, L.H., Eisenhardt, K.M., Xin, K.R.: Exploring the black box: An analysis of work group diversity, conflict, and performance. Adm. Sci. Q. **44**(1), 1–28 (1999)
20. Prieto, I.M., Revilla, E., Rodriguez-Prado, E.: Managing the knowledge paradox in product development. J. Knowl. Manage. **13**, 157–170 (2009)
21. Ryu, S., Ho, S.H., Han, I.: Knowledge sharing behavior of physicians in hospitals. Exp. Syst. Appl. **25**(1), 113–122 (2003)
22. Silander, T., Myllymäki, P.: A simple approach for finding the globally optimal Bayesian network structure. In: Proceedings of 22nd Conference on Uncertainty in Artificial Intelligence, July 13–16, (2006)
23. Senge, P.M.: The Fifth Discipline: The Art and Practice of the Learning Organization. Doubleday, New York (1990)
24. Staples, D.S., Webster, J.: Webster: Exploring the effects of trust, task interdependence and virtualness on knowledge sharing in teams. Inform. Syst. J. **18**, 617–640 (2008)
25. Taylor, A., Greve, H.R.: Superman or the fantastic four? Knowledge combination and experience in innovative teams. Acad. Manage. J. **49**(4), 723–740 (2006)
26. Tiwana, A., Mclean, E.R.: Expertise integration and creativity in information systems development. J. Manage. Inform. Syst. **22**(1), 13–43 (2005)
27. West, M.A.: Sparkling fountains or stagnant ponds: An integrative model of creativity and innovation implementation in work groups. Appl. Psychol. Int. Rev. **51**, 355–424 (2002)
28. Williams, W.M., Yang, L.T.: Organizational creativity. In: Sternberg, R.J. (ed.) Handbook of Creativity, pp. 373–391. Cambridge University Press, Cambridge, England (1999)
29. Woodman, R.W., Sawyer, J.E., Griffin, R.W.: Toward a theory of organizational creativity. Acad. Manage. Rev. **18**(2), 293–321 (1993)

Chapter 8
A Longitudinal Analysis of Team Creativity Evolution Patterns Based on Heterogeneity and Network Structure: An Approach with Agent-Based Modeling

Do Young Choi, Kun Chang Lee, and Young Wook Seo

8.1 Introduction

Creativity has recently attracted wide attention from organizations because it is a strategic source of competitiveness and organizations can use creativity to expedite innovation and enhance performance in an increasingly competitive market. Research on the relation between creativity and its influencing factors has spanned the individual, team, and organizational levels [1, 2]. Considering that the activities and tasks of organizations are usually conducted in the context of a team environment, the strategic importance of team-level creativity and its influencing factors (contextual and social factors) will be increasingly significant. In order to analyze the effect of creativity at the team level, various factors should be considered when focusing on a social context perspective [1, 3]. In other words, we should examine how the characteristics and the social context of teams, including team size, diversity, heterogeneity, cohesiveness, task characteristics, organizational structure, and social network structure among members, affect team creativity.

The purpose of this research is to longitudinally explore the evolutionary pattern of team creativity in order to explain how team characteristics and social factors affect team creativity based on the perspective of a social network structure and resource characteristics. Although various factors can be considered when addressing team

D.Y. Choi
LG CNS Co. Ltd, Seoul 100-725, Republic of Korea
e-mail: dychoi96@gmail.com

K.C. Lee(✉)
Department of Interaction Science, SKK Business School, Sungkyunkwan University,
Seoul 110-745, Republic of South Korea
e-mail: kunchanglee@gmail.com

Y.W. Seo
Software Engineering Center at National IT Industry Promotion Agency,
Seoul 138-711, Republic of Korea
e-mail: seoyy123@gmail.com

K.C. Lee (ed.), *Digital Creativity: Individuals, Groups, and Organizations*,
Integrated Series in Information Systems 32, DOI 10.1007/978-1-4614-5749-7_8,
© Springer Science+Business Media New York 2013

creativity, this research mainly focuses on one resource characteristic–heterogeneity– and two social network factors–degree centrality and structural holes. In order to address the research question stated above, we conducted experiments and simulations on how the patterns of team creativity evolve over time from the perspective of heterogeneity and network structure with agent-based modeling (ABM). While previous studies on team creativity have generally focused on the cross-sectional analysis of the relationships between team creativity and influencing factors, this research used ABM to longitudinally analyze the team creativity evolutionary pattern. ABM is generally used as the research method in the field of social emergence and social complexity, predicting macro- or meso-level changes based on the attributes of micro-level behaviors and their interactions [4, 5]. As ABM can be used to draw significant interpretations by modeling and simulating social behaviors, we adopt ABM to analyze the evolutionary pattern of team creativity. ABM is appropriate for this research because it focuses on longitudinally analyzing the changes and patterns in team creativity based on the attributes of team members and the interactions among the team members in the social network.

8.2 Literature Review

8.2.1 Team Creativity

Creativity has been studied in various fields, and the concept of creativity differs among researchers and research areas. However, it is generally accepted that creativity is a series of processes that lead to innovative results through the ability to create something new [6]. Studies on creativity have explored the topic at the individual level as well as the team and organizational level [2]. While researchers focusing on creativity at the individual level have considered personal characteristics and cognitive capability as influencing factors, structural and social characteristics should be considered in order to address creativity at the team level [1, 3]. Factors influencing team creativity include organizational atmosphere, leadership type, organizational culture, and the organizational structure and system [7]. Teams are considered task units that conduct operations with the available resources and make decisions in order to achieve their goals. We thus consider the knowledge, skills, and expertise held by team members as significant resources related to team creativity [8].

8.2.2 Heterogeneity and Network Structure

Heterogeneity is generally considered to be a facilitator of organizational learning and team creativity [9]. However, research on the heterogeneity of teams is controversial in regard to its effect on team performance. According to the first view, the heterogeneity of a team may cause the coordination problem of social division, resulting in ineffective teamwork [10, 11]. In the second view, heterogeneity can enhance a team's performance because diverse teams can increase the capacity for creative problem solving [12].

Regarding the network structure, a network is a type of social capital that can increase efficiency and collaboration through the exchange of information among nodes in its structure [13]. There are two different perspectives considering the network to be social capital: network density and structural hole. While Coleman [14] stressed that networks with higher density can increase trust and collaboration among members, Burt [15] introduced the concept of the structural hole, which is a non-duplicated relationship between two nodes that can increase efficiency and effectiveness for network operations. Accordingly, Burt [15] insisted that teams within loosely coupled networks could exchange non-duplicated information and then achieve network efficiency with the advantage of a strong mediator. Several other researchers studied team creativity from the perspective of the network structure, stressing that the interactions among team members and the social environment could enhance innovative work products within organizations [9, 16–18]. Uzzi and Spiro [16] addressed how collaboration and creativity among team members could enhance team performance based on the relational strength and cohesiveness under a small world network, and Balkundi and Harrison [17] stressed that teams with higher density could achieve their goals more effectively. Tsai [19] showed that teams with higher network centrality could increase access to information quality and accordingly could adapt more efficiently complex tasks and complicated knowledge. According to Reagans et al. [20], organizations with more structural holes could enhance their potential capability to create new knowledge and innovation, and could then increase team creativity through structural holes.

8.3   Research Methods and Experimental Results

8.3.1   Research Framework and Methods

Team creativity tends to evolve differently depending on the heterogeneous characteristics of team members (a resource of the organization) and the network structure, which determines the interactions among team members regarding information and knowledge. In other words, team creativity can be affected by the diversity of team members, and at the same time, the degree centrality and structural holes can influence team creativity revelation processes from the perspective of the network structure. In this sense, the research framework focused on in this paper regarding the effects of team heterogeneity and network structure on the evolution of team creativity is represented in Fig. 8.1.

In order to conduct simulation experiments, we designed an agent-based creativity simulator (ABCS) using NetLogo 4.1.2 (available at http://ccl.northwestern.edu/netlogo) as shown in Fig. 8.2.

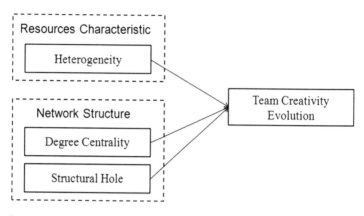

Fig. 8.1 Research framework

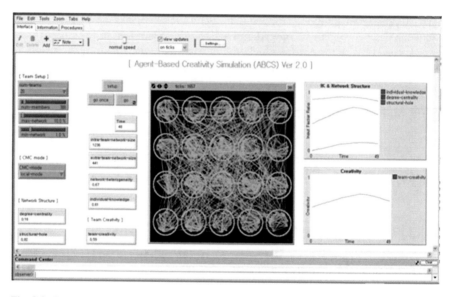

Fig. 8.2 Experimental environment: agent-based creativity simulator (ABCS)

The simulation environment and assumptions we made are as follows. First, regarding the team environment in the experiment, we designed 20 teams within an organization with a total of 300 members. Each member was assigned to one of 20 teams, each of which had a different number of team members. By doing this, we could get various changes in degree centrality and structural holes. Second, in order to vary the heterogeneity, we made the teams differ in terms of normally distributed heterogeneity, with tenure randomly assigned to the team members. After 200 simulations, teams were divided into two groups based on median value (0.499): teams with high heterogeneity (HH) and teams with low heterogeneity (LH). Third, the network structure among the team members was designed to be randomly created in each simulation. Furthermore, the network relations randomly increased or decreased at every time-lag to explore the effect of the network structure over time. In order to examine the longitudinal effects of degree centrality and structural hole, teams were divided based on two kinds of degree centrality and structural hole after 160 simulations, as before in the heterogeneity: (1) teams with high degree centrality (HDC) and those with low degree centrality (LDC); and (2) teams with high structural holes (HSH) and those with low structural holes (LSH).

In order to design the ABM model for team creativity, heterogeneity, degree centrality, and structural holes, we adapted measures based on the reliable literature. In the case of team creativity, we adapted the functions developed by Lazaric and Raybaut [21].[1] To determine the heterogeneity of a team, we used the functions defined by Reagans and Zuckerman [9].[2] For the two social network indexes—centrality degree and structural hole—we referred to Batallas and Yassine [22][3] and Soda et al. [23][4], respectively.

---

[1] Research defined by team creativity ($K_i(t)$) as a function of (1) the activation level of efforts ($e_i(t)$), (2) cumulative knowledge within teams (μ_i), and (3) interactions among members and teams (ξ_i) is based on the functions of Lazaric and Raybaut [21]: $K_i(t) = \lambda_i e_i(t)$, $\lambda_i = \mu_i + \xi_i$.

[2] Heterogeneity could be calculated based on the proportion of i's interactions with j on team k (p_{ijk}), and the degree of tenure similarity between i and j (w_{ijk}).

$$nh_{ik} = 1 - \sum_{j=1}^{N_k} w_{ijk} \times p_{ijk}$$

$$NH_k = \left(\frac{\sum_{i=1}^{n_k} nh_{ik}}{N_k} \right)$$

[3] Degree centrality is defined as follows:

$$C'_D(n_i) = d(n_i) = \sum \forall_{j \neq i} x_{ij} / (n-1)$$

$d(n_i)$ refers to the number of relations hold by member i, and x_{ij} is 1 if member i is indicent to member j, and 0 otherwise.

[4] We used the constraint and structural hole defined by Soda et al. [23]:

$$c_{ij} = \left(p_{ij} + \sum_{q=1}^{n} p_{iq} \times p_{qj} \right)^2,$$

Where $i^1 j$, p_{ij} is the proportion of i's relations invested in contact j, and *structural hole* could be calculated as $1 - C$.

8.3.2 Experimental Results

A total of 200 simulations were conducted from time-lag 1 to time-lag 48. Figure 8.3 shows the pattern for the average value of team creativity over time in regard to heterogeneity and degree centrality. We compared four situations: teams with high heterogeneity and high degree centrality (HH-HDC), teams with high heterogeneity and low degree centrality (HH-LDC), teams with low heterogeneity and high degree centrality (LH-HDC), and teams with low heterogeneity and low degree centrality (LH-LDC). The results of the four patterns show that team creativity gradually increases over time. However, team creativity tends to gradually decrease after a certain time lag. These results agree with previous research indicating that an increase in network density can enhance trust and collaboration among members within the network, resulting in a positive effect on team creativity and performance. On the other hand, a high network density may also have high coordination costs, resulting in a negative effect on team performance [9, 17]. Therefore, team creativity tends to gradually decrease above a certain point of degree centrality even though it keeps increasing. As shown in Fig. 8.3, teams with high heterogeneity can keep a higher creativity level than those with lower heterogeneity. However, we found other patterns when considering degree centrality. In early time lags, teams with HH-LDC have a lower level of team creativity than those with LH-HDC. In the long term viewpoint, the pattern show that teams with high degree centrality(HH-HDC, LH-HDC) have a higher level of team creativity than those with low degree centrality(HH-LDC, LH-LDC). Therefore, we can infer that although heterogeneity is a significant factor for team creativity, the network structure, or degree centrality, can be a more significant factor in the long term.

Figure 8.4 shows the patterns of team creativity over time in regard to heterogeneity and structural holes. Four types of graphs are shown for analysis: teams with high heterogeneity and high structural holes (HH-HSH), teams with high heterogeneity and low structural holes (HH-LSH), teams with low heterogeneity and high structural holes (LH-HSH), and teams with low heterogeneity and low structural holes (LH-LSH). The results of the four patterns show that team creativity gradually increases over time. However, team creativity tends to gradually decrease after a certain time lag, as with degree centrality. We can interpret this result as teams with higher structural holes having the advantage of a strong mediator and an accordingly higher level of team creativity through increased network efficiency and effectiveness. However, above a certain level of the structural hole, the structural hole may decrease network efficiency and effectiveness. As shown in Fig. 8.4, teams with high heterogeneity can keep a higher creativity level than those with lower heterogeneity, as in the degree centrality case. However, we found contrasting results when considering structural holes. In early time lags, teams with high heterogeneity (HH-HSH, HH-LSH) have higher levels of team creativity than those with low heterogeneity(LH-HSH, LH-LSH). However, the pattern in the long term shows that teams with high structural holes (HH-HSH, HH-LSH) have higher levels of team creativity than those with low structural holes (HH-LSH, LH-LSH).

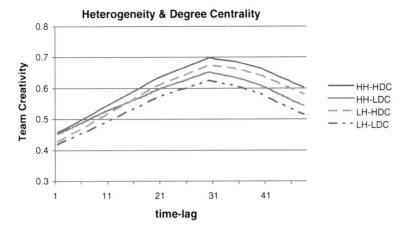

* HH = High Heterogeneity, LH = Low Heterogeneity, HDC = High Degree
  Centrality, LDC = Low Degree Centrality

Fig. 8.3 Team creativity patterns by heterogeneity and degree centrality. *HH* high heterogeneity, *LH* low heterogeneity, *HDC* high degree centrality, *LDC* low degree centrality

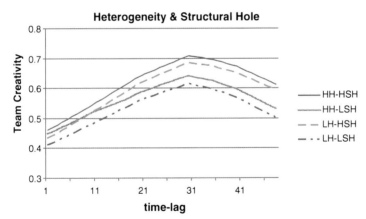

* HH = High Heterogeneity, LH = Low Heterogeneity, HSH = High Structural
  Hole, LSH = Low Structural Hole

Fig. 8.4 Team creativity patterns by heterogeneity and structural hole. *HH* high heterogeneity, *LH* low heterogeneity, *HSH* high structural hole, *LSH* low structural hole

Therefore, we can infer that although heterogeneity is a significant factor for team creativity, the network structure, or structural holes, can be more significant in the long term, as in the case of degree centrality.

The statistical verification of each group's longitudinal creativity patterns is as follows Fig. 8.1 summarizes the simulation results over time in Figs. 8.3 and 8.4.

Table 8.1 also represents the mean value of each group's creativity and rank among the four groups on time-lag 1, time-lag 15, time-lag 30, and time-lag 48.

In addition, we analyzed the mean values of the groups' team creativity utilizing ANOVA with SPSS 13.0 in order to verify whether there was a statistically significant difference among the groups from the perspective of the time lag. We analyzed the statistical differences among four groups from the perspective of heterogeneity and degree centrality in regard to the mean value of team creativity on time-lag 1, time-lag 15, time-lag 30, and time-lag 48: a group (or teams) with high heterogeneity (HH), a group with low heterogeneity (LH), a group with high degree centrality (HDC), and a group with low degree centrality (LDC). The statistical differences among four groups from the heterogeneity and structural hole perspective were also tested in the same way: a group with high heterogeneity (HH), a group with low heterogeneity (LH), a group with HSH, and a group with LSH. The ANOVA results are summarized in Tables 8.2 and 8.3.

First, when we consider the test of the homogeneity of variances as seen in Table 8.2, the significance levels of heterogeneity and degree centrality at four time points—time-lag 1, time-lag 15, time-lag 30, and time-lag 48—are 0.164, 0.321, 0.447, and 0.332, respectively. The significance levels of heterogeneity and structural holes at the same four time points are 0.103, 0.116, 0.215, and 0.339, respectively. These results indicate that the variances in the population are the same, as all of the significance levels exceed 0.05.

Second, the ANOVA results in Table 8.3 show that the significance values of each group at the four time points—time-lag 1, time-lag 15, time-lag 30, and time-lag 48—exceed 0.05, indicating that the mean values of team creativity among HH, LH, HDC, LDC differ, and HH, LH, HSH, LSH also show differences from the perspective of the mean values of team creativity.

Furthermore, a Scheffe post hoc test was conducted in order to investigate which combinations of groups have pairwise differences. The results are summarized in Table 8.4. When we consider differences between heterogeneity and degree centrality, the group with high heterogeneity and the group with low heterogeneity differ at time-lag 1, time-lag 15, and time-lag 30. However, the group with high degree centrality and the group with low degree centrality differ at time-lag 30 and time-lag 48. The group with high heterogeneity and the group with low heterogeneity differ at time-lag 1, time-lag 15, and time-lag 30 when heterogeneity and structural holes are considered. At the same time, there are differences between the group with HSH and the group with LSH. However, at time-lag 48, the group with HSH differs from the group with LSH.

8.4 Discussion

In the pattern analysis through ABM simulations, both heterogeneity and network structure (degree centrality and structural holes) were found to positively affect team creativity. Furthermore, degree centrality and structural holes were found to be

Table 8.1 Summary of simulations results

	Group		Mean of team creativity				Ranking
			Time-lag = 1	Time-lag = 15	Time-lag = 30	Time-lag = 48	
H & DC (Fig. 8.3)	① HH	HDC	0.4569	0.5846	0.6977	0.6008	Time-lag 1: ① > ② > ③ > ④
	② HH	LDC	0.4507	0.5565	0.6515	0.5423	Time-lag 15: ① > ② > ③ > ④
	③ LH	HDC	0.4261	0.5578	0.6745	0.5801	Time-lag 30: ① > ② > ③ > ④
	④ LH	LDC	0.4181	0.5277	0.6244	0.5129	Time-lag 48: ① > ② > ③ > ④
H & SH (Fig. 8.4)	① HH	HSH	0.4603	0.5913	0.7073	0.6112	Time-lag 1: ① > ② > ③ > ④
	② HH	LSH	0.4472	0.5495	0.6414	0.5307	Time-lag 15: ① > ② > ③ > ④
	③ LH	HSH	0.4327	0.5667	0.6856	0.5934	Time-lag 30: ① > ② > ③ > ④
	④ LH	LSH	0.4113	0.5191	0.6139	0.5005	Time-lag 48: ① > ② > ③ > ④

H heterogeneity, *DC* degree centrality, *SH* structural hole, *HH* high heterogeneity, *LH* low heterogeneity, *HDC* high degree centrality, *LDC* low degree centrality, *HSH* high structural hole, *LSH* low structural hole

Table 8.2 Test of homogeneity of variances

	Time-lag	Levene statistic	df1	df2	Sig.
H & DC	1	1.720	3	196	0.164
(Fig. 8.3)	15	1.173	3	196	0.321
	30	0.890	3	196	0.447
	48	1.144	3	196	0.332
H & SH	1	2.087	3	196	0.103
(Fig. 8.4)	15	1.997	3	196	0.116
	30	1.504	3	196	0.215
	48	1.127	3	196	0.339

H heterogeneity, *DC* degree centrality, *SH* structural hole

more effective than heterogeneity in the long term. That is, although teams with high heterogeneity showed higher levels of team creativity than those with lower heterogeneity in the early periods of the simulation, teams with high values on the network structure index tended to have higher levels of team creativity in the long term. In the experiments, we found that network structures such as degree centrality and structural holes were more effective factors in influencing team creativity than heterogeneity over the long term, although heterogeneity was also significant.

There are several implications of the current study for managers in order to improve team creativity. First, managers should consider designing teams to include various types of expertise, tenure, knowledge, and skills among the team members. Under a heterogeneous working environment, team members can enhance team creativity by sharing information and developing new knowledge, and accordingly improve the team's performance. Second, managers should strategically deal with the social network structure in order to enhance team creativity over the long term. Although teams have abundant resources to reach their goals, an efficient and effective network structure among teams and organizations should be managed to achieve improved performance because the activities and tasks of teams are typically conducted in the context of a team-based work environment.

8.5 Concluding Remarks

In this research we found that heterogeneity and network structure (degree centrality and structural holes) affect team creativity over time through time-dependent simulations with the ABM method. In order to analyze the effect of influencing factors, we divided teams into several groups based on their heterogeneity, degree centrality, and structural holes. Through the pattern analysis, we found that both heterogeneity and network structure positively affect team creativity, as found previously in the literature. However, we found that the network structure (degree centrality and structural holes) is more effective in the long term. Therefore, organizations and managers should focus on the network structure from a long-term perspective in terms of the organizational design and management.

Table 8.3 ANOVA table

	Time-lag	Groups	Sum of squares	df	Mean square	F	Sig.
H & DC	1	Between groups	0.052	3	0.017	38.541	0.000***
		Within groups	0.088	196	0.000		
		Total	0.140	199			
	15	Between groups	0.078	3	0.026	26.001	0.000***
		Within groups	0.195	196	0.001		
		Total	0.273	199			
	30	Between groups	0.143	3	0.048	27.620	0.000***
		Within groups	0.338	196	0.002		
		Total	0.481	199			
	48	Between groups	0.224	3	0.075	29.361	0.000***
		Within groups	0.498	196	0.003		
		Total	0.721	199			
H & SH	1	Between groups	0.065	3	0.022	56.896	0.000***
		Within groups	0.075	196	0.000		
		Total	0.140	199			
	15	Between groups	0.135	3	0.045	64.403	0.000***
		Within groups	0.137	196	0.001		
		Total	0.273	199			
	30	Between groups	0.264	3	0.088	79.554	0.000***
		Within groups	0.217	196	0.001		
		Total	0.481	199			
	48	Between groups	0.404	3	0.135	83.377	0.000***
		Within groups	0.317	196	0.002		
		Total	0.721	199			

H heterogeneity, *DC* degree centrality, *SH* structural hole

***p < 0.001

Table 8.4 Result of post hoc test (Scheffe)

	Time-lag	Group 1	Group 2	Sig.	Difference
H & DC	1	1(HH-HDC)	2(HH-LDC)	0.549	x
			3(LH-HDC)	0.000**	o
			4(LH-LDC)	0.000**	o
		2(HH-LDC)	3(LH-HDC)	0.000**	o
			4(LH-LDC)	0.000**	o
		3(LH-HDC)	4(LH-LDC)	0.317	x
	15	1(HH-HDC)	2(HH-LDC)	0.000**	o
			3(LH-HDC)	0.001**	o
			4(LH-LDC)	0.000**	o
		2(HH-LDC)	3(LH-HDC)	0.998	x
			4(LH-LDC)	0.000**	o
		3(LH-HDC)	4(LH-LDC)	0.000**	o
	30	1(HH-HDC)	2(HH-LDC)	0.000**	o
			3(LH-HDC)	0.053*	o
			4(LH-LDC)	0.000**	o
		2(HH-LDC)	3(LH-HDC)	0.050**	o
			4(LH-LDC)	0.015**	o
		3(LH-HDC)	4(LH-LDC)	0.000**	o
	48	1(HH-HDC)	2(HH-LDC)	0.000**	o
			3(LH-HDC)	0.244	x
			4(LH-LDC)	0.000**	o
		2(HH-LDC)	3(LH-HDC)	0.003**	o
			4(LH-LDC)	0.039**	o
		3(LH-HDC)	4(LH-LDC)	0.000**	o
H & SH	1	1(HH-HSH)	2(HH-LSH)	0.012**	o
			3(LH-HSH)	0.000**	o
			4(LH-LSH)	0.000**	o
		2(HH-LSH)	3(LH-HSH)	0.003**	o
			4(LH-LSH)	0.000**	o
		3(LH-HSH)	4(LH-LSH)	0.000**	o
	15	1(HH-HSH)	2(HH-LSH)	0.000**	o
			3(LH-HSH)	0.000**	o
			4(LH-LSH)	0.000**	o
		2(HH-LSH)	3(LH-HSH)	0.015**	o
			4(LH-LSH)	0.000**	o
		3(LH-HSH)	4(LH-LSH)	0.000**	o
	30	1(HH-HSH)	2(HH-LSH)	0.000**	o
			3(LH-HSH)	0.015**	o
			4(LH-LSH)	0.000**	o
		2(HH-LSH)	3(LH-HSH)	0.000**	o
			4(LH-LSH)	0.001**	o
		3(LH-HSH)	4(LH-LSH)	0.000**	o
	48	1(HH-HSH)	2(HH-LSH)	0.000**	o
			3(LH-HSH)	0.164	x
			4(LH-LSH)	0.000**	o
		2(HH-LSH)	3(LH-HSH)	0.000**	o
			4(LH-LSH)	0.003**	o
		3(LH-HSH)	4(LH-LSH)	0.000**	o

H heterogeneity, *DC* degree centrality, *SH* structural hole, *HH* high heterogeneity, *LH* low heterogeneity, *HDC* high degree centrality, *LDC* low degree centrality, *HSH* high structural hole, *LSH* low structural hole
*$p < 0.1$, **$p < 0.05$

This research has several contributions to both theory and practice. First, we addressed team creativity and its influencing factors using a new research method, ABM. This approach provides an important foundation for future research and expands the literature on team creativity. Second, we investigated the longitudinal effect of factors influencing team creativity, while previous research has mainly focused on cross-sectional analyses. Third, we provide implications for practice from the experimental evidence that the network structure, such as degree centrality and structural holes, may be more important to consider in the long term. There are also a few limitations of the current research. First, we conducted only 200 simulations for the experiment, which is not enough to generalize the results. Second, we considered only degree centrality and structural holes among several network structure indexes in order to explore the effect of the network structure, although there may be several other measures of team characteristics. Future researchers should expand this work by using various network structure indexes and attributes. Third, we could enhance the reality of the ABM simulation results conducted in this study by applying other research methods, including empirical analysis.

Acknowledgments This work was supported by the Korea Research Foundation Grant funded by the Korean Government (KRF-2009-342-B00015). Also this research was partially supported by WCU (World Class University) program through the National Research Foundation of Korea funded by the Ministry of Education, Science, and Technology (Grant No. R31-2008-000-10062-0).

References

1. Amabile, T.M.: A model of creativity and innovation in organizations. Res. Organ. Behav. **10**, 123–167 (1988)
2. Ancona, D.G., Calewell, D.F.: Demography and design: Predictors of new product team productivity. Organ. Sci. **3**, 321–341 (1992)
3. Andriopoulos, C.: Determinants of organizational creativity: A literature review. Manage. Decis. **39**(10), 834–840 (2001)
4. Balkundi, P., Harrison, D.A.: Ties, leaders, and time in teams: Strong inference about the effects of network structure on team viability and performance. Acad. Manage. J. **49**, 49–68 (2006)
5. Batallas, D.A., Yassine, A.: Information leaders in product development organizational networks: Social network analysis of the design structure matrix. IEEE Trans. Eng. Manage. **53**(4), 570–582 (2006)
6. Brand, A.: Knowledge management and innovation at 3M. J. Knowl. Manage. **2**(1), 17–22 (1998)
7. Burt, R.S.: Structural Holes: The Social Structure of Competition. Harvard University Press, Cambridge, MA (1992)
8. Coleman, J.: Foundations of Social Theory. Harvard Business Press, Cambridge (1990)
9. Kogut, B.: The network as knowledge: Generative rules and the emergence of structure. Strat. Manage. J. **21**(3), 405–425 (2000)
10. Kurtzberg, T.R., Amabile, T.M.: From Guilford to creative synergy: Opening the blackbox of team-level creativity. Creativ. Res. J. **13**, 285–294 (2001)
11. Lazaric, N., Raybaut, A.: Knowledge creation facing hierarchy: The dynamics of groups inside the firm. J. Artif. Soc. Soc. Simulat. **7**(2) 2004

12. Milgram, R.M., Rabkin, L.: Developmental test of Mednick's associative hierarchies of original thinking. Dev. Psychol. **16**, 157–158 (1980)
13. North, M.J., Macal, C.M.: Managing Business Complexity: Discovering Strategic Solutions with Agent-Based Modeling and Simulation. Oxford University Press, New York (2007)
14. O'Reilly III, C.A., Caldwell, D.F., Barnett, W.P.: Work group demography, social integration, and turnover. Admin. Sci. Q. **34**, 21–37 (1989)
15. Pfeffer, J.: Organizational demography: Implications for management. Calif. Manage. Rev. **28**, 67–81 (1983)
16. Reagans, R.E., Zuckerman, E., McEvily, B.: How to make the team: Social networks vs. demography as criteria for designing effective teams. Adm. Sci. Q. **49**(1), 101–133 (2004)
17. Reagans, R.E., Zuckerman, E.W.: Networks, diversity, and productivity: The social capital of corporate R&D teams. Organ. Sci. **12**, 502–517 (2001)
18. Sawyer, R.K.: Social Emergence: Societies as Complex Systems. Cambridge University Press, New York (2005)
19. Soda, G., Usai, A., Zaheer, A.: Network memory: The influence of past and current networks on performance. Acad. Manage. J. **47**(6), 893–906 (2004)
20. Sterngerg, R.J., Lubart, T.I.: Defying the Crowd, Cultivating creativity in a culture of conformity. The Free Press, New York (1995)
21. Tsai, W.: Social capital, strategic relatedness and the formation of intra-organizational linkages. Strat. Manage. J. **21**, 925–939 (2000)
22. Uzzi, B., Spiro, J.: Collaboration and creativity: The small world problem. Am. J. Sociol. **111**, 447–504 (2005)
23. Woodman, R.W., Sawyer, J.E., Griffin, R.W.: Toward a theory of organizational creativity. Acad. Manage. Rev. **18**(2), 293–321 (1993)

Chapter 9
Examining the Effect of Short-Term Robot-Mediated Training for Creativity Education

Jungsik Hwang and Kun Chang Lee

9.1 Introduction

Creativity is considered to be one of the most essential and required abilities for individuals, and many previous studies have shown the importance of creativity. For example, creative individuals were reported to be more productive and satisfied with their occupation [1]. In addition, Walton [2] found that almost 80% of managers considered creativity as the most important factor for occupational success.

The definitions of creativity in the literature vary somewhat. According to [3], two widely used definitions of creativity exist: the first focuses on idea generation or problem solving [1], and the second focuses on the mental process of generating new and innovative ideas [4]. Although many factors have been reported to be involved in the creativity process, five dimensions of creativity have gained the most attention among researchers: divergent thinking, attitudes and interests, personality traits, biographical inventories, and creative accomplishments [2].

Many training programs have been developed and employed to enhance individual creativity since evidence of the importance of creativity was provided by researchers. In particular, robot-mediated creativity training has recently gained attention. Several researchers [5–10] have reported the effectiveness of robot-mediated training for individual creativity and the advantages of using robots for education. For example, robots are fascinating to people, especially for children [6].

Therefore, the present research focuses on examining the effect of short-term robot-mediated training for creative education. As creativity is often measured by

J. Hwang
Department of Interaction Science, Sungkyunkwan University,
Seoul, Republic of Korea
e-mail: jungsik.hwang@gmail.com

K.C. Lee (✉)
Department of Interaction Science, Business School, Sungkyunkwan University,
Seoul, Republic of South Korea
e-mail: kunchanglee@gmail.com

K.C. Lee (ed.), *Digital Creativity: Individuals, Groups, and Organizations*,
Integrated Series in Information Systems 32, DOI 10.1007/978-1-4614-5749-7_9,
© Springer Science+Business Media New York 2013

self-assessment and evaluation of creative outcomes [11], we investigated the effect of robot-mediated training on improving creative self-efficacy and producing creative outcomes. Creative self-efficacy [12, 13] refers to a belief that one is able to produce creative outcomes and is believed to impact individual creativity [14]. Therefore, the research questions in the present research are:

1. Does short-term robot-mediated training help people to improve creative self-efficacy?
2. Does short-term robot-mediated training help people to produce more creative outcomes?

The remainder of the paper is organized as follows. In Section 2, we briefly review previous works related to robot-mediated creativity education. The experimental setup is then introduced in Section 3, with the results of the experiment presented in Section 4. The implications are discussed in Section 5 and the paper concludes in Section 6.

9.2   Related Works

Since technology was introduced in the field of education, robots have been adopted to promote individual creativity. Several previous studies have introduced robot-mediated creativity education and demonstrated its effectiveness. According to [6], robots possess several advantages in education. For example, robots are attractive to people and are multidisciplinary systems.

The Thymio robot discussed in [6] was presented in workshops during a robotic festival to promote students' creativity and learning. Children played with the Thymio robot and built different types of robots using Thymio. The authors argued that the Thymio robot partly fulfilled the goal of promoting creativity. Xuemei and Gang [9] introduced the modular robot platform, which was designed to develop creativity, and argued that the experience of using and developing robot platforms offered the opportunity for students to develop creativity. Another widely used robot platform for creative education is Lego Mindstorms [15]. Due to its flexible characteristics, several previous researchers [5, 10] have used Lego Mindstorms to investigate individual creativity. Other previous researchers have used a variety of robots, such as the e-puck robot [8] and HangulBot [7], both of which showed the effectiveness of using robots for creativity education.

The majority of previous researchers employed the concept of experimental learning, which was described as "the process whereby knowledge is created through the transformation of experience" in [16]. Therefore, the students were able to promote creativity while engaging in robot-related tasks. In addition, student creativity can be developed by experiencing experimental activities [17].

This paper is in line with the previous research discussed above. There are, however, several distinctive features in the present study as compared with previous

Fig. 9.1 A dinosaur-like robot, Pleo

studies. First, we investigate the effect of short-term robot-mediated training for improving an individual's creative self-efficacy. Second, we also examine whether robot-mediated training could help people to produce more creative outcomes.

9.3 Experiment

9.3.1 Robot

A dinosaur-like robot (Fig. 9.1) from Innvo Labs [18], Pleo, was used in the present experiment. Pleo contains several actuators and sensors inside that allow it to interact with people. Pleo is particularly focused on the modality of touch. That is, the touch sensors embedded within Pleo's body enable the robot to interact with people through touch.

9.3.2 Experimental Conditions

In order to investigate the effect of robot-mediated training on promoting individual creativity, three conditions were examined: watching Pleo-related movie clips, playing with Pleo, and designing Pleo's behaviors. The participants were randomly assigned into one of three conditions.

In the watching Pleo-related movie clips condition (C1), Pleo was not presented but the participants watched nine video clips related to Pleo, such as PLEO advertisements and user created content (UCC) about PLEO. The total length of all video clips was approximately 20 min. In the playing with Pleo condition (C2), Pleo was

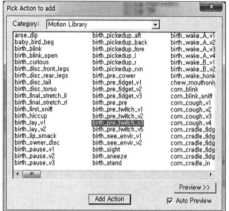

Fig. 9.2 User interface of the Yet Another Pleo Tool (YAPT)

presented and the participants were asked to play with Pleo for 20 min. In order to make the participants focus on interacting with Pleo, we provided participants with an instruction sheet and asked them to observe the robot's behavior by following the instructions. Pleo's response to each type of touch was previously manipulated in order to provide the same reaction for each participant. In the designing Pleo's behavior condition (C3), participants were asked to design Pleo's behavior using Yet Another Pleo Tool (YAPT) for 15 min. YAPT [19] is a choreography tool used to edit Pleo's movement. Due to its simple user interface, the participants were able to easily design Pleo's behavior. Figure 9.2 illustrates the user interface of YAPT. After being given 15 min to design Pleo's behavior, Pleo was presented and the participants observed Pleo's behavior (designed by himself/herself) for 5 min.

9.3.3 Measurements

Creative Self-Efficacy. Thirteen items previously used in [20] were utilized in order to measure participants' creative self-efficacy. Examples of the items were: I often have a fresh approach to problems; and I often have new and innovative ideas. Creative self-efficacy was measured both before and after the experiment. The items were presented in Likert scale format and the participants were asked to indicate their responses from 1 (strongly disagree) to 1 (strongly agree). The Cronbach's alpha for the pretest measure was 0.87 and that for the posttest measure was 0.91.

Creative Outcome. In order to examine the effect of robot-mediated training on producing creative outcomes, we asked the participants to complete a writing task related to Pleo. The participants were told that the writings would be used to teach children. In addition, we informed the participants that there was no limitation in writing so that they could write any creative stories they wanted. The writing task consisted of three steps: suggesting topics, writing emotional expressions about each topic, and writing short stories based on the topic they suggested. Participants' writings were assessed by six experts who have worked in the field of creativity. The scores ranged from 1 (the lowest) to 7 (the highest).

9.3.4 Participants

A total of 34 students (13 females and 21 males) from a large private university were recruited for the experiments. The average age of the participants was 23.1 years with a standard deviation of 2.8. The participants were from a variety of majors, such as business, engineering, and so on. The majority of the participants reported that they had no previous experience using Pleo or the YAPT program.

9.3.5 Procedure

The online pretest questionnaire was presented to the participants 1 week before the experiment began. Upon arrival at the experiment room, the participants signed an informed consent form. Next, a brief introduction about Pleo was presented to the participants. After the introduction, the main experiment began. For 20 min, the participants watched Pleo-related movie clips, played with Pleo, or designed Pleo's behavior using YAPT (according to their experimental condition). After the experiment, a writing task was assigned to the participants. Thirty minutes were assigned for the writing task. After the writing task, the participants were given the posttest questionnaire. After completing the posttest questionnaire, the participants left the experimental room.

9.4 Result

The Kruskal–Wallis and Mann–Whitney tests were employed to examine the effect of robot-mediated training on both improving creative self-efficacy and producing creative outcomes. All statistical analyses were performed using PASW Statistics (formerly SPSS Statistics) 18.

9.4.1 Effect of Robot-Mediated Training on Creative Self-Efficacy

The improvement in creative self-efficacy was calculated by subtracting the scores on the pretest questionnaire from the scores on the posttest questionnaire.

Table 9.1 Descriptive statistics for an improvement in creative self-efficacy

	Condition	Mean	Median	S.D.	Max	Min
Improvement in creative self-efficacy	Watching Pleo-related videos (C1)	−0.11	−0.08	0.45	0.46	−0.85
	Playing with Pleo (C2)	0.12	0.08	0.33	0.62	−0.38
	Designing Pleo's behavior (C3)	0.27	0.23	0.41	1.15	−0.31

Table 9.1 shows the descriptive statistics for creative self-efficacy. Next, the Kruskal–Wallis test was conducted to examine the differences in improvement in creative self-efficacy among the three conditions. The results revealed that there was no statistically significant difference among the three conditions ($\chi^2=3.51$, $p=0.17$, df = 2). However, the Mann–Whitney test for comparing two conditions [watching Pleo-related videos (C1) and designing Pleo's behavior (C3)] showed marginally significant results. Table 9.2 shows the results of the Mann–Whitney test.

9.4.2 Effect of Robot-Mediated Training on Producing Creative Outcomes

The participants' writings about Pleo were assessed by six creativity experts. The highest and lowest scores for each participant were excluded, and the remaining scores were averaged for each participant. Table 9.3 shows the descriptive statistics for the writing assessment. The average writing score was calculated by averaging the three scores from each writing step (W1, W2, and W3). The Kruskal–Wallis test was then conducted to examine the differences in participants' writing scores among the three conditions. The results revealed a statistically significant difference for writing emotional expressions (W2: $\chi^2=8.21$, $p=0.02$, df = 2). No significant results were found for writing topics (W1: $\chi^2=2.50$, $p=0.29$, df = 2) or writing short stories (W3: $\chi^2=0.63$, $p=0.73$, df = 2). We also made pairwise comparisons (Mann–Whitney test, Table 9.4) and found a marginally significant difference between two conditions (C1 and C3). We did not report the comparison results of C2 (playing with Pleo) with the other two conditions because no statistically significant differences were found.

9.5 Discussion

The results from Section 4.1 show the effect of robot-mediated training in improving an individual's creative self-efficacy. Compared to the group of participants who watched Pleo-related movie clips (C1), there was a significantly higher improvement in creative self-efficacy for participants who actually

Table 9.2 Mann–Whitney test results for an improvement in creative self-efficacy

	Condition	N	Mean rank	Sum of ranks
Improvement in creative self-efficacy	Watching Pleo-related videos (C1)	11	9.27	102.00
	Designing Pleo's behavior (C3)	12	14.50	174.00
	Mann–Whitney $U(2)=36.00$, $Z=-1.85$, $^*p=0.07$			

Table 9.3 Descriptive statistics for the assessment of participants' writings

	Condition	Mean	Median	S.D.	Max	Min
Writing score	Watching Pleo-related videos (C1)	4.42	4.33	0.60	5.58	3.42
	Playing with Pleo (C2)	3.96	4.17	0.74	5.00	2.58
	Designing Pleo's behavior (C3)	3.81	3.75	0.68	5.17	2.83

Table 9.4 Mann–Whitney test results for the assessment of participants' writings

	Condition	N	Mean rank	Sum of ranks
Writing score	Watching Pleo-related videos (C1)	11	14.91	164.00
	Designing Pleo's behavior (C3)	12	9.33	112.00
	Mann–Whitney $U(2)=34.00$, $Z=-1.97$, $^{**}p=0.05$			

designed the robot's behavior. This result is in line with several previous studies [5, 9] showing the effectiveness of experimental learning for creativity education. Charyton and Merrill [17] argued that creativity can be developed by experiencing experimental activities. Therefore, the experience of designing and observing a robot's behavior in the experiment may have increased the participants' creative self-efficacy.

Regarding creative outcomes, however, different results were found. The participants who actually designed the robot's behavior received lower scores than participants who watched the robot-related movie clips. This result could be explained by the concept of creative writing. Creative writing can be defined as the production of fictional stories [21], and the writing task assigned to participants during the experiment could be considered to be creative writing. According to [22], six main factors are related to creative writing: general knowledge and cognition, creative cognition, executive functioning, motivation and other conative characteristics, linguistic and literary, and psychomotor. Therefore, it can be assumed that the participants gained more knowledge about Pleo when watching movie clips than when designing Pleo's behavior. Consequently, the participants in C3 produced more creative pieces of writing. In addition, other factors such as writing abilities and fluency may have affected the outcomes.

In sum, we found that the short-term robot-mediated training session was effective for improving creative self-efficacy, but it did not necessarily predict creative outcomes (i.e., creative writing). This result is somewhat contradictory to previous studies [13, 14] showing a direct relationship between creative self-efficacy and creative performance. The duration of the present experiment was relatively short, and it is expected that long-term robot-mediated training for creativity education would possibly elicit increases in both creative self-efficacy and the production of creative outcomes.

9.6 Concluding Remarks

The present research investigated the effect of short-term robot-mediated training on individual creativity. A dinosaur-like robot was used for the creative training session. Regarding creativity, two goals (improving creative self-efficacy and producing creative outcomes) were examined. The results indicated that participants who designed the robot's behavior had greater improvements in creative self-efficacy. However, the participants who watched robot-related video clips received higher scores in the assessment of creative outcomes (writings) as compared with the participants who designed the robot's behavior.

A few research directions are suggested based on the results of the present research. First, the effect of long-term robot-mediated training for improving creative self-efficacy should be investigated. Second, the relationship between creative self-efficacy and creative performance when using robots should be further researched.

Acknowledgments This work was supported by the Korea Research Foundation Grant funded by the Korean Government (KRF-2009-342-B00015). This research was also partially supported by WCU (World Class University) program through the National Research Foundation of Korea funded by the Ministry of Education, Science, and Technology (Grant No. R31-2008-000-10062-0).

References

1. Amabile, T.M.: The Social Psychology of Creativity. Springer, New York (1983)
2. Walton, A.P.: The impact of interpersonal factors on creativity. Int. J. Entrepr. Behav. Res. **9**, 146–162 (2003)
3. Klijn, M., Tomic, W.: A review of creativity within organizations from a psychological perspective. J. Manage. Dev. **29**, 322–343 (2010)
4. Mayer, R.E.: Fifty years of creativity research. In: Sternberg, R.J. (ed.) Handbook of Creativity, pp. 449–460. Cambridge University Press, Cambridge (1999)
5. Jenyi, C.: The effects of LEGO Mindstorms on indigenous students' creativity in Taiwan—A case study of an Energy and Robotics Course. In: IEEE 2011 International Conference on Electrical and Control Engineering (ICECE), pp. 6907–6910, Yichang, China, 16-18 September (2011)
6. Riedo, F., Rétornaz, P., Bergeron, L., Nyffeler, N., Mondada, F.: A two years informal learning experience using the thymio robot. In: Rückert, U., Joaquin, S., Felix, W. (eds.) Advances in Autonomous Mini Robots, pp. 37–48. Springer, Berlin, Heidelberg (2012)
7. Kwak, S.S., Eun Ho, K., Jimyung, K., Youngbin, S., Inveom, K., Jun-Shin, P., Eun Wook, L.: Field trials of the block-shaped edutainment robot HangulBot. In: 2012 7th ACM/IEEE International Conference on Human-Robot Interaction (HRI), pp. 403–403, Boston, Massachusetts, USA, 5-8 March (2012)

8. Bonani, M., Raemy, X., Pugh, J., Mondana, F., Cianci, C., Klaptocz, A., Magnenat, S., Zufferey, J.C., Floreano, D., Martinoli, A.: The e-puck, a Robot Designed for Education in Engineering. Proceedings of the 9th Conference on Autnomous Robot Systems and Competitions 1, pp. 59–65, IPCB, Castelo Branco, Portugal, 7 May (2009)

9. Xuemei, L., Gang, X.: Interdisciplinary innovative education based on modular robot platform. In: Computing, Communication, Control, and Management, 2008. CCCM '08. ISECS International Colloquium on, pp. 66–69, Guangzhou, China, 3-4 August (2008)

10. Nagchaudhuri, A., Singh, G., Kaur, M., George, S.: LEGO robotics products boost student creativity in precollege programs at UMES. In: Frontiers in Education, 2002. FIE 2002. 32nd Annual, pp. S4D-1-S4D-6 vol.3, Stipes Publishing LLC, Boston, Massachusetts, USA, 6-9 November (2002)

11. Smith, D.K., Paradice, D.B., Smith, S.M.: Prepare your mind for creativity. Commun. ACM **43**, 110–116 (2000)

12. Bandura, A.: Self-Efficacy: The Exercise of Control. Freeman, New York (1997)

13. Tierney, P., Farmer, S.M.: Creative self-efficacy: Its potential antecedents and relationship to creative performance. Acad. Manage. J. **45**, 1137–1148 (2002)

14. Seo, Y.W., Chae, S.W., Lee, K.C.: The impact of creative self-efficacy, IT support, and knowledge on individual creativity through absorptive capacity. In: Kim, T.-H., Adeli, H., Ma, J., Fang, W.-C., Kang, B.-H., Park, B., Sandnes, F.E., Lee, K.C. (eds.) U- and E-Service, Science and Technology, vol. 264, pp. 177–186. Springer, Berlin, Heidelberg (2011)

15. Lego Mindstorms, http://mindstorms.lego.com. Accessed 25 Aug 2012

16. Kolb, D.A.: Experiential Learning: Experience as the Source of Learning and Development. Prentice Hall Inc, New Jersey (1984)

17. Charyton, C., Merrill, J.A.: Assessing general creativity and creative engineering design in first year engineering students. J. Eng. Educ. **98**, 145–156 (2009)

18. PLEOworld, http://www.pleoworld.com. Accessed 25 Aug 2012

19. YAPT (Yet Another Pleo Tool), http://www.aibohack.com/pleo/yapt.htm Accessed 25 Aug 2012

20. Zhou, J., George, J.M.: When job dissatisfaction leads to creativity: Encouraging the expression of voice. Acad. Manage. J. **44**, 682–696 (2001)

21. Nettle, D.: The evolution of creative writing. In: Kaufman, S.B., Kaufman, J.C. (eds.) The Psychology of Creative Writing, pp. 101–116. Cambridge University Press, New York (2009)

22. Barbot, B., Tan, M., Randi, J., Santa-Donato, G., Grigorenko, E.L.: Essential skills for creative writing: Integrating multiple domain-specific perspectives. Think. Skills Creativ. **7**(3), 209–223 (2012)

Chapter 10
Towards the "Digital Creativity of Action"

Teresa Swirski

10.1 The Foundations of the Digital Creativity of Action

Depending upon your stance, as to what exactly forms the basis of creativity may easily illicit a dozen answers, as well as incite score more questions. The reason creativity can be so contentious is its multidimensional facets—with varying discourses, practices, and "rhetorics" [4]. The interpretation chosen to frame this chapter is that creativity is situated in our actions, as well as reflexive and contextual [2, 8, 12, 25]. By acknowledging how central creativity is to our everyday lives, we can begin to increase understandings regarding our capacities to be creative. That is, awareness of what we know, how we act and who we are becoming can be conceptualized as dynamic and creative possibilities—rather than static and predetermined precepts. Exploring our creative abilities to shape social practices accepts creativity and improvisation as "intrinsic to the very processes of social and cultural life" ([22], p. 19). Such a perspective foregrounds the inherent relationship between creativity and the dynamic formation of social practice. This premise invites an exploration of what constitutes the foundations of the "digital creativity of action"—an investigation of the expanding role which digital technologies have to play amongst our social practices.

10.2 Background

In recent years, social computing has impacted upon all aspects of our personal, professional, and social lives: "Over the last decade, information and communication technologies have enabled changes in the way people live, work, interact and acquire

T. Swirski (✉)
Charles Sturt University, Sydney, NSW, Australia
e-mail: tswirski@csu.edu.au

K.C. Lee (ed.), *Digital Creativity: Individuals, Groups, and Organizations*,
Integrated Series in Information Systems 32, DOI 10.1007/978-1-4614-5749-7_10,
© Springer Science+Business Media New York 2013

knowledge" ([1], p.3). How these new technologies interrelate with creativity and social practices to *create* change is the focus of this paper. Subsequently, the understanding of "digital creativity of action" introduced in this chapter is described as:

> the imaginative ways we improvise via new technologies and innovate our social practices; this involves an interplay between the structures of what we know, the occasions in which we interact, as well as the practices of who we are becoming.

Stemming from this, digital creativity is introduced as an embodied, enacted, and emergent practice. This complexity perspective explores how our social practices are shaped by—and shape—the ways in which we imagine, improvise, and innovate [35]. The circumstances amongst which digital creativity is situated influences our current and future practices. Embodied practices are characterized by complexity, where new constructs, "wicked problems" [31] and rapid changes require imaginative thinking. These new ways of thinking inform how digital creativity is enacted—the ways in which we improvise practices through the multimodality of new technologies. Such innovations shape the expansion of "lifewide learning" [5]—the evolving spaces of digital creativity which blur the traditional borders and boundaries of formal and informal learning.

This conceptualization of the "digital creativity of action" builds upon a phenomenographic analysis of the ways in which students, academics, and professionals conceptualized creativity [35]. Findings from this study (Table 10.1) revealed the qualitatively different ways these groups experienced creativity. Dimensions of variation (embodied, enacted, and emergent) represent a range of conceptions of creativity. These categories of description illustrate the limited to broad ways in which creativity can be experienced. Reading a phenomenographic outcome space as a hierarchical relationship assists to see how broader categories of creativity are inclusive of the other categories.

These findings provide the foundation for the conceptualization of "digital creativity of action" advanced in this chapter. Exploring the interrelationship between creativity, technology, and social practice seeks to inform future studies of digital creativity; that is, the situations which shape our embodied, enacted, and emergent practices. The prominent creativity theorist Csikszentmihalyi [13] maintains that "the task of a good society is not to enshrine the creative solutions of the past into permanent institutions; it is, rather, to make it possible for creativity to keep asserting itself" (p. 276).

Through exploring the dimensions of "digital creativity of action," the author seeks to introduce a term which has implications for how professionals, educators and researchers critically reflect upon how creative practices are evolving. Increasing awareness of how digital creativity is embodied, enacted, and emergent provides a lens for further examining how social practices are being transformed. In his book "Beyond the Stable State" Schön [32] suggests that we must:

> become adept at learning, We must become able not only to transform our institutions, in response to changing situations and requirements; we must invent and develop institutions [and societies] that are "learning systems", that is to say, systems capable of bringing about their own continuing transformation. (p. 30)

Table 10.1 Phenomenographic outcome space findings: dimensions of variation

Dimensions of variation	Creativity is "embodied"		Creativity is "enacted"		Creativity is "emergent"	
	1	2	3	4	5	6
Categories of description ↑	Peripheral	Personal	Collaborative	Societal	Liminal	Transformative
Students	Disconnected	Intuitive	Interactive	Real-world	Challenging	Fusion
Academics	Constrained	Contextual	Brokering	Engaging	Risk-taking	Fluidity
Professionals	Reactive	Valuable	Networking	Crossing boundaries	Evolving	Futures

As new digital technologies become increasingly integrated amongst social practices, the question for professionals, educators and researchers is not so much "Why is creativity even important?" ([34], p. 7). Rather, the question to pose is this—why is *digital* creativity even important?

10.3 Embodied Practices of Digital Creativity

A study of the embodied, enacted, and emergent ways in which students, academics, and professionals conceptualize creativity [35] highlighted the ways in which conceptions of creativity can be peripheral, personal, collaborative, societal, liminal, and transformative. These findings illustrate the variation in the possible ways that creativity can be experienced. This provides the basis for opening up a discussion about the role that digital technologies play in relation to creativity and social practices.

A complexity perspective can inform our understanding of the way in which the practices of digital creativity are embodied, enacted, and emergent. These dynamic interrelationships which characterize complexity have been informed by theories such as nonlinear dynamics and systems thinking [10, 11]. This recognizes the plurality of contexts, processes, and spaces which interweave amongst our social practices. Fenwick [19] describes how:

> Complexity theory interrupts the natural tendency to seek clear lines between figures and grounds, and focuses on the relationships binding humans and non-humans (persons, material objects, mediating tools, environments, ideas) together in multiple fluctuations in complex systems. (p. 5)

An understanding of digital creativity as an embodied practice is crucial within "global complexity" [37]. Amidst a "runaway world" [20] our conceptions of tradition and stability are dissonant with the way in which society has so rapidly evolved—requiring a new framing of how professional identities and social practices are formed. This suggests what Bauman [6] terms "liquid modernity" which highlights the more pronounced flux and flow of modern life—providing a more nuanced lens from more finite sociological inquiries. Social practices have always been interwoven; however, acknowledging complexity unveils the intensity of modern "global cultural flows"—technoscapes, ethnoscapes, mediascapes, financescapes, and ideoscapes [3]. These overlapping "scapes," or territories have heightened the intensity with which our local–global lives are embodied amongst continually evolving technologies, social patterns, communications, economics and ideologies.

To reduce the risk of paralysis within our "risk society" [7] there is an urgency to understand more about how we can increase our capacities to deal with these new and complex situations. The digital creativity of action does not claim to be a panacea for the world's problems; what it does claim is that personal and collaborative practices can be transformed amidst lifewide learning through the shaping of new technologies. Increasing awareness of how individuals and groups can *imagine* new technologies may enhance their sense of agency and wellbeing.

> Our social imaginary at any given time is complex. It incorporates a sense of the normal expectations that we have of each other; the kind of common understanding which enables us to carry out the collective practices which make up our social life. This incorporates some sense of how we all fit together in carrying out the common practice. This understanding is both factual and "normative"; that is, we have a sense of how things usually go, but this is interwoven with an idea of how they ought to go, of what mis-steps would invalidate the practice. ([36], p. 18)

The role of the imagination within a complex society gains importance if we acknowledge that agency is central to social practice. Foregrounding the understanding that individuals and groups not only interrelate, interact — but initiate and invent as well — can increase awareness of our creative capacities. Dall'Alba [14] maintains:

> Central to Heidegger's ontology is his concept of "being-in-the-world", which emphasises that we are always already embedded in, and entwined with, our world, not simply contained within it. As Heidegger points out, we typically are absorbed in a range of activities and projects with others that involve the use of tools or equipment and production of artefacts. (p. 35)

The understanding that creativity is systemic, or componential [2, 12, 13] aligns with a complexity theory approach. Professional identity and knowledge is formed from the juxtaposition of what one knows from the past, with the judgment of how to act in the present:

> … professional knowledge is mismatched to the changing characteristic of the situations of practice — the complexity, uncertainty, instability, uniqueness, and value conflicts which are increasingly perceived as central to the world of professional practice. ([33], p.14)

How professionals embody the challenges of these changing situations interweaves with their enacted and evolving practices. Amidst complexity and with the diverse range of new technological tools at hand — what are the novel personal and collaborative practices which professionals can imagine? *The digital creativity of action promotes the idea that how we imagine new technologies is shaping and transforming the embodied structures of what we know.*

10.4   Enacted Practices of Digital Creativity

Understandings that creativity was "interactive," "brokering," and "networking" corresponded to the collaborative category of a phenomenographic analysis of creativity [35]. The adjoining category where participants viewed creativity as societal suggested that they had more of an awareness, or understanding of creativity — it was "real-world," "engaging," and "crossing boundaries." This enacted dimension of creativity suggests that people's conceptions of creativity were strongly shaped by their associations with others. These findings provide a rich foundation for exploring the ways in which *digital* creativity is enacted in our social practices.

The processes of digital creativity are enacted through the multiple modes, or mediums, of new technologies. Based upon text, images, sound, and gestures, there is an ever increasing array of diverse combinations and complex arrangements with which we improvise and express ourselves:

> In the new theory of representation, in the context of the multimodal, multimedia modes of textual production in the era of electronic technologies, the task of text-makers is that of complex orchestration. Further, individual are now seen as remakers, transformers, of sets of representational resources—rather than as users of stable systems, in a situation where a multiplicity of representational modes are brought into textual compositions. ([26], p. 160)

Resonating with a complexity perspective, creativity is articulated in the literature as being universal, "mini-c," everyday and part of the evolving self [8, 13, 24, 30]. In accordance with complexity theory, if creativity is embodied in our practices—it follows that it is enacted and evolving as well. Amidst the new technologies, or the multimodality, which have become part and parcel of our everyday lives, these novel expressions have become increasingly entwined with how we express ourselves. As such, digital technologies are enabling the potential for personal and collaborative creativity. Redecker [29] states how:

> Social computing applications acknowledge the fact that learning processes are increasingly characterized by *collaboration and networking*. One of the main assets of these tools is therefore their potential to promote and increase collaboration, empowering the individual as a producer, but at the same time embedding his creative potential in a network of mutual assistance and support (p. 82)

Supporting this notion, Burgess' [9] term "vernacular creativity" encapsulates the spirit of how creativity has become part of our everyday discourse and practice.

The "digital creativity of action" I have introduced in this chapter expands upon Joas' [25] phrase "the creativity of action." This social theorist perspective which views creativity as being situated, is still very much laden within the term. However, what has been added is the word "digital"—highlighting how the practices of creativity have expanded alongside emerging digital technologies. The "digital creativity of action" does not assume that all actions are creative, it emphasizes that there is creative potential which has been enhanced through digital technologies; this has enabled not only past actions but immediate and prospective actions as well. This poses:

> the question of what the social order would look like that *we* should create, and want to create, *for ourselves*. Now that there are no longer any metasocial guarantees to underpin the creation of social orders, reflection causes us to turn to the creativity of human action itself. ([25], p. 258)

As with Joas' [25] creativity of action, the *digital* creativity of action similarly posits our agency and capacity to create, or improvise. The creativity of action does not function passively. Nor does the digital creativity of action operate in simple reaction to new technologies. Both forms of creativity are enacted in their possibilities—the capacity to draw upon our imaginations, improvisations and innovations. Creativity is central to human agency if it is conceptualized:

> as a temporally embedded process of social engagement, informed by the past, (in its habitual aspect), but also oriented toward the future (as a capacity to imagine alternative

possibilities) and toward the present (as a capacity to contextualize past habits and future projects with the contingencies of the moment) ([18], p. 963)

As with creativity in general, digital creativity cannot be guaranteed, or prescribed. The practices of what we know, how we act and who we are becoming—left to their own devices—can still be a dormant and uncreative process. It is only through fostering *creative agency* that personal and collaborative practices are able to be transformed. Eisler [17] states how:

> We humans are the most creative life forms on our planet—amazing beings who can change not only our environments but also ourselves. With a clearer understanding of who we are, what we can be, and what is needed for a more sustainable, equitable, and peaceful global culture, we can use our enormous creativity to construct foundations for truly civilized cultures. As cocreators of our future, we can build cultures in synch with the direction of evolution toward the consciousness, caring, and creativity that are the true hallmarks of being human. (p. 282)

The processes of the "digital creativity of action" are therefore not indiscriminate. The creation of new technologies, how we choose to shape them, and what we select to innovate further—is a process of devising new artifacts. This process is a form of *improvising*—that is, working with the potential multimodalities and communicative range of new technologies. As a professional, it is through enactment that novel personal and collective practices are devised according to new situations and complex arrangements. The practices of jazz musicians highlight the creativity of such arrangements: "Improvisation consists in varying, combining, and recombining a set of figures within the schema which bounds and gives coherence to the performance" ([33], p. 55).

How professionals improvise with new technologies—through the expressive multimodality of texts, images, sound, and gesture—comprises not only the processes but also the possibilities of digital creativity. *The digital creativity of action suggests that our improvisation with new technologies is shaping and transforming the occasions in which we enact, or interact.*

10.5   Emerging Practices of Digital Creativity

The broadest categories of description relating to a phenomenographic study of creativity [35] were "liminal" and "transformative." Within the liminal category of description, creativity was viewed as "challenging," "risk-taking," and "evolving." Characterizing the transformative category of description were the ideas of creativity as involving "fusion," "fluidity," and "futures." These findings suggest that creativity is not something simply we "know" or "do"—creativity involves who we are becoming. Creativity involves choices and decisions which directly impact upon our current and future practices. This study illustrated how creativity is not simply an isolated action, or event; rather, creativity operates on a continuum of possible experiences. This has strong implications upon how we arrange our environments and the ways in which creativity is enabled or constrained. As such, this provides a strong foundation for exploring the interactions between creativity, social practices and technology.

The digital creativity of action is characterized by evolving practices which correspond with the concept *lifewide* learning. This shift towards the richness, nuances and wellbeing of learning takes place across the spectrum of formal and informal learning: "Lifewideness is fundamentally concerned with the way we create, engage with, sense, and make sense of our own experiences" ([23], p. 7). These lifewide characteristics similarly inform the evolving characteristics of professional identity and social practice. Dall'Alba and Barnacle [15] indicate how a more dynamic perspective of professional identity corresponds with changes in practice:

> In order to achieve a shift in focus to developing ways of being, what it means to be(come) a teacher, artist, physicist, historian, engineer, architect, and so on, must be a central and ongoing question that continues to be addressed explicitly throughout (and beyond) higher education programmes. Becoming is, by definition, never complete. Instead, what it means to be(come) a teacher, etc., is dynamic and changing over time with developments in practice, and the place of particular forms of practice in society more generally. (p. 687)

In relation to new technologies, how professionals innovate and shape these artifacts influences the formation and creation of their social practice. These dynamic principles of becoming a professional and lifewide learning resonate with Beghetto and Kaufman's [8] articulation of "mini-c creativity":

> the novel and personally meaningful interpretation of experiences, actions, and events … information is not simply transmitted from the environment and passively received without any alteration. Rather, people filter and interpret information through the lens of their existing conceptions, personal histories, and past experiences. (p. 73)

In recent years the profile of creativity as a desired capability has increased within both professional and educational domains; this has sparked interest in how such lifewide learning can be fostered. For instance, IBM's [21] Global Student Study states: "Like CEO's, six out of ten students rated creativity among the top three leadership qualities, more than any other attribute" (p. 2). Such expectations of employees and students provoke new insights into how a curriculum or workplace which fosters creativity may be arranged. In their book "Educating the creative workforce," McWilliam and Haukka [28] posit how:

> educators have both the opportunity and challenge of shifting their attention from content delivery to *capacity building*, from supplying curriculum, to *co-creating* curriculum, from supplying education to *navigating learning networks*. In so doing, they will help young people to shift their attention from their own individual performance to their capacity to learn through their own networks—to connect, access information, and forge relationships in and through dynamic and productive teams. (p. 663)

How professional identities and social practices evolve are central to a complexity perspective: the interweaving of what we know, how we act, and who we are becoming. The shape of these evolving practices can be traced to an enacted practice, whose threads are recalled from an embodied practice. Soon these innovations become mainstreamed—and even habit; thereby making way for new and novel practices. In "The Reflective Practitioner" Schön [33] suggests how:

> In a practitioner's reflective conversation with a situation that he treats as unique and uncertain, he functions as an agent/experiment. Through his transaction with the situation, he shapes it makes himself a part of it. Hence, the sense he makes of the situation must include his own contribution to it. Yet he recognizes that the situation having a life of its own distinct from his intentions, may foil his projects and reveal new meanings. (p. 163)

The innovations of digital technologies which are integrated in social practice evolve from how professionals have imagined and improvised with these new artifacts. This complex arrangement of these contexts, processes, and spaces comprise the "assemblages" [16] from which personal and collaborative practices become transformed. *The digital creativity of action suggests that through innovating new technologies we are shaping and transforming the emerging practices of who we are becoming.*

10.6   The Future of the "Digital Creativity of Action"

The theoretical argument advanced in this chapter built upon an empirical, phenomenographic analysis of the ways in which students, academics, and professionals conceptualize creativity. Exploring the emergent, enacted, and evolving dimensions of digital creativity then became the subsequent focus of this chapter. Emphasizing the processes of digital creativity as *action*—that is, as a situated and dynamic practice—highlights how digital creativity influences the ways in which we learn, interact with others, and engage with the world at large:

> "Digital creativity of action" is the imaginative ways we improvise via new technologies and innovate our social practices; this involves an interplay between the structures of what we know, the occasions in which we interact, as well as the practices of who we are becoming.

In this chapter I explored how Joas' [25] term "the creativity of action" has become—within modernity—the "digital creativity of action." This proposition stems from the initial understanding of creativity as being implicit in our everyday, situated actions. However, if we acknowledge the increasing influence of technologies upon our social practices, then this notion requires advancement: from which the addition to and introduction of the term "*digital* creativity of action" emerges.

Our complex society has been intensified through the modern iteration of globalization, sparking new inquiry into the formation of individual identities and social patterns. Similarly, there has been a marked diversification of available expressions for multimodality which has expanded how we interact and collaborate through text, visuals, sound, gesture, and speech. How we learn—both formally and informally— has also been significantly impacted by increasing confluence of digital technologies and knowledge environments. The illustration of creativity explored in this chapter sought to highlight how a newly emerging "digital creativity of action" is contributing towards the shaping and transformation of our social practices. Through this creative agency, the practices of individuals, groups, and organizations will continue to evolve as new technologies emerge—remaining an ongoing focus for creative, cultural, and educational studies. However, amidst this "imaginative act" [27] another aspect which requires equal attention amongst professionals, educators and researchers is: *how* should digital creativity evolve? A normative impetus invites us to critically reflect upon not just how we create, but also for what purpose—and to what end? Shifting a scholarly lens upon *the ethicality of digital creativity* is a provocation for future interdisciplinary creativity research. As Eisler [17] suggests:

> We can choose to be passive. Or we can use our creativity to create cultures that are in synch with today's requirements for human survival and with the direction of evolution towards ever greater consciousness, caring, and creativity. (p. 262)

References

1. Ala-Mutka, K., Punie, Y., Redecker, C.: ICT for learning, innovation and creativity. European Commission, Joint Research Centre, Institute for Prospective Technological Studies. http://ftp.jrc.es/EURdoc/JRC48707.TN.pdf (2008). Accessed 2 Feb 2012
2. Amabile, T.M.: Creativity in Context. Westview Press, Boulder (1996)
3. Appadurai, A.: Modernity at Large. University of Minnesota Press, Minneapolis (2003)
4. Banaji, S., Burn, A., Buckingham, D.: The Rhetorics of Creativity: A Review of the Literature. Arts Council England, London (2007)
5. Barnett, R.: Life-wide education: A new and transformative concept for higher education. In: Jackson, N. (ed.) Learning for a Complex World, Chapter 2, pp. 22–38. AuthorHouse, Bloomington (2011)
6. Bauman, Z.: Liquid Modernity. Polity, Cambridge (2000)
7. Beck, U.: Risk Society: Towards a New Modernity. Sage Publications, London (1992)
8. Beghetto, R.A., Kaufman, J.C.: Toward a broader conception of creativity: A case for 'mini-c' creativity. Psychol. Aesthet. Creativity Arts 1(2), 73–79 (2007)
9. Burgess, J.: Hearing ordinary voices: Cultural studies, vernacular creativity and digital storytelling. Continuum J. Media Cult. Stud. 20(20), 201–214 (2006)
10. Capra, F.: The Hidden Connections: A Science for Sustainable Living. Anchor Books, New York (2002)
11. Capra, F.: The Web of Life: A New Scientific Understanding of Living Systems. Anchor Books, New York (1996)
12. Csikszentmihalyi, M.: Society, culture, and person: A systems view of creativity. In: Sternberg, R.J. (ed.) The Nature of Creativity: Contemporary Psychological Perspectives, pp. 325–339. Cambridge University Press, Cambridge (1988)
13. Csikszentmihalyi, M.: The Evolving Self. HarperCollins Publishers, Inc., New York (1993)
14. Dall'Alba, G.: Learning professional ways of being: Ambiguities of becoming. Educ. Philos. Theory 41(1), 34–45 (2009)
15. Dall'Alba, G., Barnacle, R.: An ontological turn for higher education. Stud. High. Educ. 32(6), 679–691 (2007)
16. Deleuze, G., Guattari, F.: A Thousand Plateaus. University of Minnesota Press, Minneapolis (1987)
17. Eisler, R.: Our great creative challenge: Rethinking human nature—and recreating society. In: Richards, R. (ed.) Everyday Creativity, pp. 261–285. American Psychological Association, Washington (2007)
18. Emirbayer, M., Mische, A.: What is agency? Am. J. Sociol. 103(4), 962–1023 (1998)

19. Fenwick, T.: The practice-based learning of educators: A co-emergent perspective. Scholar Pract. Q. **2**(4), 43–59 (2004)
20. Giddens, A.: Runaway World. Profile Books Ltd, London (2002)
21. IBM Institute for Business Value.: Inheriting a complex world: Future leaders envision sharing the planet. http://public.dhe.ibm.com/common/ssi/ecm/en/gbe03350usen/GBE03350USEN. PDF (2010b). Accessed 12 Jan 2012
22. Ingold, T., Hallam, E.: Creativity and cultural improvisation: An introduction. In: Hallan, E., Ingold, T. (eds.) Creativity and Cultural Improvisation, pp. 1–24. Berg, Oxford (2007)
23. Jackson, N.: The lifelong and lifewide dimensions of living, learning and developing. In: Jackson, N. (ed.) Learning for a Complex World, Chapter 1, pp. 1–21. AuthorHouse, Bloomington (2011)
24. Jeffrey, B., Craft, A.: The universalization of creativity. In: Craft, A., Jeffrey, B., Leibling, M. (eds.) Creativity in Education, pp. 1–13. Continuum, London (2001)
25. Joas, H.: The Creativity of Action. Polity Press, Cambridge (1996)
26. Kress, G.: Design and transformation: New theories of meaning. In: Cope, B., Kalantzis, M. (eds.) Multiliteracies: Literacy Learning and the Design of Social Future, pp. 153–161. Routledge, New York (2000)
27. McCarty, W.: Humanities Computing. Palgrave Macmillan, Basingstoke, UK; New York (2005)
28. McWilliam, E., Haukka, S.: Educating the creative workforce: New directions for twenty-first century schooling. Brit. Educ. Res. J. **34**(5), 651–666 (2008)
29. Redecker, C.: Review of learning 2.0 practices. European Commission, Joint Research Centre, Institute for Prospective Technological Studies. http://ftp.jrc.es/EURdoc/JRC48707.TN.pdf (2008). Accessed 2 Feb 2012
30. Richards, R.: Everyday creativity: Our hidden potential. In: Richards, R. (ed.) Everyday Creativity, pp. 25–53. American Psychological Association, Washington (2007)
31. Rittel, H., Webber, M.: Dilemmas in a general theory of planning. In: Policy Sciences, vol. 4(2), pp. 155–169
32. Schön, D.: Beyond the Stable State. Random House, New York (1971)
33. Schön, D.: The Reflective Practitioner: How Professionals Think in Action. Basic Books, New York (1983)
34. Sternberg, R.J.: The nature of creativity. Creativity Res. J. **18**(1), 87–98 (2006)
35. Swirski, T.: Becoming a creative practitioner in a complex society: Fostering a capability approach in higher education pedagogy. Unpublished thesis: Macquarie University, Sydney (2012)
36. Taylor, C. (n.d.). On social imaginary. http://blog.lib.umn.edu/swiss/archive/Taylor.pdf. Accessed 12 Jul 2011
37. Urry, J.: Global Complexity. Polity, Cambridge (2003)

Index

K.C. Lee (ed.), *Digital Creativity: Individuals, Groups, and Organizations*,
Integrated Series in Information Systems 32, DOI 10.1007/978-1-4614-5749-7,
© Springer Science+Business Media New York 2013

Printed by Publishers' Graphics LLC
BT20130401.09.07.81